BOOK THREE

Navigating the Mathematics Common Core State Standards

Decatur High School
310 N. McDonough St.
Decatur, GA 30030
404-370-4420

BOOK THREE

Navigating the Mathematics Common Core State Standards

Jan Christinson | Maryann D. Wiggs

Cathy J. Lassiter | Lori Cook

LEAD+
LEARN
PRESS

ENGLEWOOD, COLORADO

The Leadership and Learning Center
317 Inverness Way South, Suite 150
Englewood, Colorado 80112
Phone 1.866.399.6019 | Fax 303.504.9417
www.LeadandLearn.com

Published by Lead + Learn Press, a division of Houghton Mifflin Harcourt.

Library of Congress Cataloging-in-Publication Data

Navigating the mathematics common core state standards / Jan
Christinson ... [et al.].
    p. cm. — (Getting ready for the common core handbook series ; bk. 3)
    Includes bibliographical references and index.
    ISBN 978-1-935588-16-0 (alk. paper)
 1. Mathematics—Study and teaching—Standards—United States.
 2. Education—Standards—United States. I. Christinson, Jan.
    QA11.2.N376 2012
    510.71—dc23
                                                            2011049226

ISBN 978-1-935588-16-0

Printed in the United States of America

16 15 14 13 12   03 04 05 06 07 08

Contents

List of Exhibits

About the Authors

Jan Christinson is a Professional Development Associate with The Leadership and Learning Center. Jan's primary goal is to improve classroom instruction and thereby improve student learning. He conducts seminars based on two publications he coauthored, *Five Easy Steps to a Balanced Math Program* and *Student Generated Rubrics: An Assessment Model to Help All Students Succeed.* Jan has presented workshops and led breakout sessions at regional conferences, most notably for the California Mathematics Council and the ASCD (formerly the Association for Supervision and Curriculum Development). With 32 years of experience as an elementary and middle school classroom teacher, Jan brings a wide and varied range of educational experiences to his presentations.

With more than four decades of experience in education, **Maryann D. Wiggs** brings an abundance of expertise and wisdom to her presentations, ensuring that teachers and administrators gain practical strategies for enhancing instructional performance. As the former Assistant Superintendent of Curriculum and Instruction and Executive Director of Learning Services in two Colorado school districts, Maryann has been instrumental in orchestrating the alignment of all aspects of the leaders' and teachers' work to improve the quality of instruction in the classroom, including alignment of standards, assessment, curriculum, instruction, interventions, supervision, and evaluation. Maryann is a former speech pathologist, special and general education teacher, behavior consultant, and teacher leader, having served learners at the elementary, middle, high school, and college levels.

Cathy J. Lassiter is a Professional Development Associate with The Leadership and Learning Center. She brings a sense of passion and energy to her work on school leadership, accountability, data, curriculum, instruction, and standards. She has worked with superintendents, state departments of education, principals, and teachers to improve leadership and instructional practices. Over the course of her 28 years in public education, Cathy was a successful middle and high school teacher working primarily with urban students. She also served in numerous leadership positions including middle school principal, project manager for federal programs, director of curriculum, instruction and staff development leader, and executive director of nine middle schools. Cathy has also taught courses in educational leadership at The George Washington University.

Lori Cook is a Professional Development Associate with The Leadership and Learning Center. Lori's passion is to help teachers perfect classroom instruction, which ultimately improves student learning and performance. In a national school system, Lori trained teachers in secondary mathematics, learning environments, and the improvement of school culture. She has trained both new and veteran teachers across the country with one basic premise—that all students can understand and become successful in math. In this capacity, she also created, edited, and revised professional development instructional materials to assist future trainers. Lori has a decade and a half of classroom experience helping low-performing students find hope, resolve, and ultimately success in the classroom.

Introduction

The Leadership and Learning Center has served at the forefront of advancing best practices in implementation of standards and assessment for nearly two decades. In continuation of the pursuit of excellence in implementing the Common Core State Standards (CCSS), The Leadership and Learning Center is pleased to provide this series of four handbooks on *Getting Ready for the Common Core*. Handbooks, by design, are practical guides for "doing it yourself" and/or for rechecking one's work and "doing over" things that can be improved upon. This third handbook, *Navigating the Mathematics Common Core State Standards,* turns the reader's attention from the "what" to the "how," effectively taking the words off the page of the standards document and demonstrating explicitly how to implement the Common Core State Standards for Mathematics in classrooms across the country. As experts committed to improving education across the United States, Professional Development Associates from The Center gathered together to design this handbook to serve as a "guide on the side" for leaders and teachers as they respond to the call to action to implement the rigorous expectations outlined in the mathematics Common Core.

This handbook starts the journey of *Navigating the Mathematics Common Core State Standards* with an examination of the rigorous expectations awaiting high school mathematics students. Author and math educator Lori Cook provides readers with an explanation of the design of the high school mathematics standards, which are organized into conceptual categories. Lori's chapter on "The 'New' High School Mathematics" provides compelling arguments for the unprecedented need in this country to "ramp up" the rigor in high school mathematics programs to effectively prepare students with the understanding and skills they must have to solve the mathematically complex real-world problems required for success in post-secondary college, careers, and citizenship. Lori discusses Appendix A of the mathematics standards document, which maps out a number of possible pathways for teaching the high school mathematics standards in order to create aligned sequences of courses leading students toward preparedness upon graduation from high school.

Chapter Two is about learning progressions, one of the powerful design and organizational features of the CCSS. Authored by Jan Christinson, the chapter focuses on "How the K–8 Learning Progressions Influence Planning for Instruction and Assessment." The chapter opens with a definition of learning progressions and provides evidence that supports the learning progressions as an intentional design feature of the standards document. Several learning progressions are illustrated that demonstrate the integrated nature of mathematics. Jan provides a succinct summary of the major features of each of the highlighted K–8 mathematics learning progressions and points out the building blocks that cross multiple domains. The chapter concludes with a series of planning questions for leaders and educators.

Chapter Three, also authored by Jan Christinson, highlights the research behind the inclusion of the standards for mathematical practice in the CCSS document. This chapter provides clear guidance for the classroom teacher on "Integrating the Standards for Mathematical Practice with the Standards for Mathematical Content." Jan is a "teacher's teacher," and as such he takes care to define complex mathematical concepts in a user-friendly fashion that provides guidance for teachers on how to thoughtfully implement these practices in the classroom. In this chapter, Jan not only defines each of the eight mathematical practice standards, but also communicates in vivid detail what will be required to implement those practices in the classroom in order to create an environment that fosters student success with mathematics.

Author Cathy Lassiter has written several chapters for the *Getting Ready for the Common Core* handbook series, all with a focus on strategies for "closing the rigor gap" found in our nation's classrooms. In this chapter on "Strategies for Addressing Rigor in the Mathematics Common Core," Cathy once again grounds readers with the research behind the drive to "close the rigor gap" in preparing our young people for their future in college or careers. Lassiter's work focuses on criteria for creating worthwhile mathematical problems to solve, which stimulates higher-level thinking and significant math development. She outlines three specific teaching strategies that will help increase rigor in the mathematics classroom.

Finally, the handbook's appendices offer "at-a-glance" information for busy mathematics educators about the critical focus areas of the Common Core, standards that integrate language skills, standards that require solving word problems, standards that call for solving real-world and mathematical problems, standards that are good points of intersection between the practice standards and content standards, the high school modeling standards, and the advanced mathematics standards.

Each handbook on *Getting Ready for the Common Core* focuses on a unifying theme to provide leaders and educators with the rationale and tools for navigating the terrain of implementing the CCSS. The first handbook in this series provides guidance for leaders in examining the leadership aspects of creating a rigorous school culture that allows *all* students to thrive in demonstrating proficiency of the Common Core State Standards. The second handbook provides specific strategies for navigating the English language arts CCSS, while this third handbook provides explicit guidance for navigating the mathematics CCSS. The fourth handbook in the series focuses on using formative assessment processes with Common Core implementation, as well as on strategies for using Professional Learning Communities and Data Teams practices as continuous improvement structures to ensure sustainability of the Common Core State Standards.

The Common Core provides an unprecedented opportunity to foster increased collaboration among teachers and increased success among students throughout the nation. So set your navigation system toward rigor, fasten your seat belt, and let's get started!

MARYANN D. WIGGS, 2011
Colorado Springs, Colorado

The "New" High School Mathematics

Lori Cook

Increasingly, the computer will do the computation ... (but) thinking about the problem, developing the problem, understanding the problem, looking at it from all sides, deciding what important information is relevant to the problem ... is the harder part.... You can't do that without an understanding of the computation.

—Achieve (2004)

The age of technology deceives students by leading them to believe that the calculator and/or computer will always produce an answer for them. Some aspects of various mathematics curricula perpetuate this misconception, leading to expectations in the United States that lag behind the expectations of other nations. Instruction often focuses on procedures instead of a true understanding of mathematics. Many U.S. students lack a deep conceptual understanding of how math works, and they are not able to apply mathematical skills and solve complex problems (National Research Council, 2001). As a result, a small percentage of students pursue science, technology, engineering, and mathematics (collectively referred to as "STEM") majors and careers.

Steve Leinwand, using the U.S. Statistical Abstract from the Census Bureau, discovered this crisis by tracking a group of students from kindergarten through graduate work in universities. Leinwand's "Pipeline Perspective" (2010) demonstrates his findings:

The Pipeline Perspective

1985: 3,800,000 kindergarten students

1998: 2,810,000 high school graduates

1998: 1,843,000 college freshmen

2002: 1,292,000 college graduates (34 percent)

2002: 150,000 STEM majors (3.9 percent)

2006: 1,200 PhDs in mathematics (0.03 percent)

In order for the United States to be a leader in these fields and the careers of the future, there is greater need for critical thinkers and problem solvers to propel our nation through the 21st century and to be successful in our global society. The National Governors Association Center for Best Practices and the Council of Chief State School Officers recognized this crisis and commissioned the Common Core State Standards Initiative (CCSSI) to position the United States as a leader in the science, technology, engineering, and mathematics fields and the jobs of the future.

At present, many states require high school students to simply complete from two to four years of mathematics in order to qualify for high school graduation (Reys, Dingman, Nevels, and Teuscher, 2007). This in itself is a difficult feat for many students, and these students are not consistently prepared for the challenges that await them in post-secondary studies and careers. It is the expectation of the authors of the Common Core State Standards and many other organizations around the country that *all* students be required to show mastery of *all* of the Common Core high school standards for mathematics. To do this, they will have to successfully complete the standards either in a traditional pathway (Algebra I, Geometry, Algebra II, with an integration of statistics and probability) or in three integrated courses that encompass the concepts and skills represented in the standards. We need to raise expectations so that our students are prepared to compete with their peers around the globe.

The Common Core documents specify that *all* students should study the subjects included in the mathematical standards so that they will be college- and career-ready (CCSSI, 2010a, p. 57). In order to achieve that goal, students must enter the course and/or grade level with mastery of the preceding standards (CCSSI, 2010a, p. 5), allowing for a rigorous curriculum. No longer will "just showing up to class" be the status quo; the Common Core requires students to show true understanding by applying the mathematics of the standards to achieve successive levels of accomplishment.

DESIGN AND ORGANIZATION

The design and organization of the high school Common Core State Standards for Mathematics are very similar to the K–8 Common Core State Standards for Mathematics. One key distinction between the K–8 standards and the high school standards is that the K–8 standards are organized by grade level and the high school standards are organized by conceptual categories. These conceptual categories represent a comprehensive view of the high school mathematics that students must understand and master to be college- and career-ready. The six conceptual categories are number and quantity, algebra, functions, geometry, statistics and probability, and modeling. Even though modeling is a conceptual category, it does not have its own set of standards; instead, modeling standards are incorporated into the other conceptual categories and are indicated by a star symbol (*) (CCSSI, 2010a, p. 57).

Each Common Core conceptual category includes an introduction summarizing the focus and level of application required of students. Definitions, expectations, learning progressions, and examples of applications are detailed within the introductions. Teachers should use each of these items while planning and preparing units of study. Even though the conceptual categories do not provide as specific a focus as the critical areas of focus that are in the K–8 standards, the introductions are very beneficial and provide insight from the CCSS authors.

Excluding modeling, the other five conceptual categories are similar in design to the K–8 standards. After the introductions (high school) and the critical areas of focus (K–8), a one-page overview outlines the domains and clusters, as well as listing the eight standards for mathematical practice for each conceptual category (high school) or grade (K–8). The overview provides a quick "snapshot" of the concepts and skills students will master. The standards for mathematical content follow the one-page overviews and are organized into domains, clusters, and standards.

Domains: Broad themes that connect topics across the grades and/or categories.

Clusters: Groups of similar standards; since the mathematics discipline is interconnected, standards from different clusters may be comparable.

Standards: What all students should know and be able to do at each grade level; expected learning outcomes.

Students should engage with the content standards by using and applying the mathematical practices. As students mature, so should their application of the practices.

The Common Core authors intended for teachers and students to find "points of intersection" between the mathematical content and practice standards, and did not narrow the possibilities of intersection by labeling standards with specific practices. "Points of intersection" between the practice standards and content standards are encouraged for, but not limited to, standards that begin with the word "understand." To truly "understand" a concept, a student must be able to "represent problems coherently, justify conclusions, apply the mathematics to practical situations, use technology mindfully to work with the mathematics, explain the mathematics accurately to other students, step back for an overview, or deviate from a known procedure to find a shortcut" (CCSSI, 2010a, p. 8). Students who do not have a balance of conceptual understanding and procedural understanding will not master the final expected outcomes.

Included throughout the high school document are standards, identified by a plus (+) symbol, that are intended to prepare students to take advanced courses such as calculus, advanced statistics, or discrete mathematics. Many states are referring to these standards as STEM (science, technology, engineering, and mathematics) standards. Even though these standards are beyond the college and career standards that all students must achieve, the authors suggest that these standards could be included within the courses designated for all students and not limited only to those students who will pursue STEM majors in post-secondary studies (CCSSI, 2010a, p. 57). The standards indicated by the plus symbol create opportunities for differentiation within the classroom and will allow students to be challenged and exposed to different topics in mathematics. By including these standards within the curriculum for all students, the CCSS authors have provided teachers with a resource to aid in accelerating student learning when appropriate.

Exhibit 1.1 lists the Common Core's conceptual categories and provides the number of college and career (CCR) standards

BOOK THREE EXHIBIT 1.1

Number of CCR and Advanced Course Work Standards

CCSS Conceptual Category	Number of CCR Standards	Number of Modeling Standards (*)	Number of Advanced Course Work Standards (+)
Number and Quantity	9	3	18
Algebra	23	8	4
Functions	22	12	8
Geometry	37	6	6
Statistics and Probability	22	31 (all)	9
Modeling	Throughout all categories		
Total:	113	60	45

Note that within the "functions" conceptual category several standards include both CCR and advanced course work standards (for example 1a* and 1b+).

(standards for all students) and the number of standards designated for advanced course work. Modeling standards can be found in both the CCR and advanced course work standards.

The Common Core State Standards for Mathematics create a viable answer to the criticism that the United States mathematics curriculum to date has been "a mile wide and an inch deep" (CCSSI, 2010a, p. 3).

APPENDIX A OF THE MATHEMATICS COMMON CORE

Since the Common Core mathematics standards for high school are organized by conceptual categories, states, districts, and/or schools are given the responsibility of creating courses that offer a solid foundation for college and career success. To assist in this effort, Achieve (in partnership with the Common Core writing team) gathered a "group of experts, including state mathematics experts, teachers, mathematics faculty from two- and four-year institutions, mathematics teacher educators, and workforce representatives to develop Model Course Pathways in Mathematics based on the Common Core State Standards" (CCSSI, 2010b, p. 2).

In no way are the courses or pathways in Appendix A intended to be directives; they are merely examples and/or models for states and districts to use as they create courses of study. The pathways provide an example of how to carefully group all of the college- and career-ready standards (standards without a "+") in such a way that all students will be positioned for post-secondary success upon high school graduation. According to the authors, "a few '+' standards are included to increase coherence, but are not necessarily expected to be addressed on high-stakes assessments"

(CCSSI, 2010b, p. 2). The groupings of the standards into courses are not intended to endorse a particular curriculum. The ordering of the units and standards also does not represent a specific sequence for instruction.

It is up to districts and schools to determine how to best implement the units based on student knowledge and needs. Similarly, the names of the units given in Appendix A are simply suggestions, and are given for organizational purposes. Even though the mathematical practices were not included within the pathways, "points of intersection" between the standards for mathematical practice and the content standards must be present in every unit of study to guarantee mathematically proficient students (CCSSI, 2010b, p. 2).

In Appendix A, four pathways are provided:

1. Traditional courses (common in the United States): Algebra I and II, and Geometry. All three courses include data, probability and statistics.

2. Integrated courses (common internationally): Course I, II, and III. All courses incorporate number, algebra, geometry, probability and statistics.

3. A "compacted" version of the traditional pathway in which no content is left out and students are able to take calculus or other college-level math courses during their senior year.

4. A "compacted" version of the integrated pathway in which no content is left out and students are able to take calculus or other college-level math courses during their senior year.

Even though the K–7 math standards prepare students for eighth-grade algebra, it is suggested that those students wishing to complete a "compacted" version complete an accelerated seventh-grade course that includes seventh-grade standards and also some of the standards from eighth grade, allowing more time to go deeply into Algebra I or Course I in eighth grade.

The compacted pathways compress the standards into shorter time intervals, but allow *all* content to be explored. The compacted pathways do *not* skip standards to accelerate students. That type of acceleration causes gaps in student learning and is not beneficial to anyone. Instead, students move through the content at a quicker pace while still including a deep implementation of the standards for mathematical practice.

Caution should be used when preparing for the acceleration of students through the standards. Even though there is a positive correlation between students who eventually take advanced mathematics courses and those who complete bachelor's degrees, there also is research showing that when certain students are pushed too quickly through mathematical topics, gaps emerge, and they are ultimately not successful in any of the mathematics topics (CCSSI, 2010b, p. 80). Each student should be evaluated carefully to make sure the correct pathway is chosen. Students' mathematical minds mature at different rates; some students take longer to truly comprehend and master the foundations of mathematics. The beautiful thing about the different pathways suggested is that all students can complete calculus by the end of their senior year even if they do not accelerate their learning in middle school (CCSSI, 2010b, p. 80). Exhibit 1.2 is an outline of the four different pathways available in Appendix A.

Common Core Mathematics Pathways

Grade Level	Traditional	Integrated	Accelerated	Double-Up
6	6	6	6	6
7	7	7	7/8	7
8	8	8	Algebra I or Course I	8
9	Algebra I	Course I	Geometry or Course II	Algebra I / Course I
10	Geometry	Course II	Algebra II or Course III	Geometry / Course II and Algebra II / Course III
11	Algebra II	Course III	Pre-Calculus	Pre-Calculus
12	(Pre-College)	Course IV	Calculus	Calculus

Each pathway is developed using a "modular" approach by grouping similar standards together, allowing the implementation of the units (critical areas; large groupings of standards) to be flexible in nature (i.e., the order in which they are taught). For example, the grouping of the standards in "Unit 1: Relationships Between Quantities and Reasoning with Equations" in the traditional pathway is identical to the groupings of standards in the integrated pathway "Unit 1: Relationships Between Quantities" minus the "Reasoning with Equations" standards (A.REI.1; A.REI.3), which are located in "Unit 3: Reasoning with Equations" within the integrated pathway. Grouping standards together in a similar fashion allows assessment teams to create assessments that can be used with the different approaches and pathways.

The authors assert that the groupings are only suggestions and encourage teams of educators in districts and schools to work together to create the best model for their students. This is a dynamic process that will need to be revisited as student performance data are collected (CCSSI, 2010b, p. 4).

MODELING

Modeling in the high school mathematics classroom is essential. The authors of the Common Core standards define modeling as "the process of choosing and using appropriate mathematics and statistics to analyze empirical situations, to understand them better, and to improve decisions" (CCSSI, 2010a, p. 72). Not only is it a standard for mathematical practice (K–12), but it also is a conceptual category within the high school standards for mathematical content. High school students who are disenchanted with the traditional mathematics approach of procedural teaching and learning are often bored or have completely given up trying to understand math. Many students ask "Why do I need to learn this?" or they may even say "What's the point? I'm not good at math." Using modeling within the mathematics classroom allows for teachers and students to "link" mathematics to the real world around them (i.e., day-to-day life, occupations, and critical thinking). In essence, modeling can be the educational "hook" that engages the students and draws them into learning experiences, and it often provides the "Aha!" moment for the student.

Descriptive modeling and analytic modeling are two types of modeling discussed within the standards. Students use descriptive modeling to portray and condense their observations or findings (often by showing data using a graph). Students use analytic modeling to explain data. These models have a "closed form" solution; that is, the solution to the equations used to describe changes in a system can be described using functions.

Focus in High School Mathematics: Reasoning and Sense Making (2009), published by the National Council of Teachers of Mathematics, suggests that using modeling within the classroom is beneficial because it does the following:

1. Shows how mathematics is connected (in life, many different mathematical strands are used to solve one problem—math is not isolated).

2. Shows students how to apply math in new and creative ways by combining mathematical concepts.

3. Engages students and encourages mathematical reasoning.

4. Creates an appropriate situation where students must not only cultivate mathematical ideas but also apply them (motivates the students).

5. Provides points of entry for students with different levels of mathematical knowledge.

Used appropriately, modeling creates the engagement needed to build connections for all students to learn and master mathematics (NCTM, 2009, pp. 13–14).

Modeling is not to be confused with the teaching strategy of showing students how to solve a problem. Instead of standing in front of the class "modeling" procedures, teachers should create opportunities for students to model, or "link," mathematics to an everyday situation. This does not need to be a complex event; it can be as simple as writing an equation representing the net profit of a company's earnings. Examples of modeling suggested in the Common Core (CCSSI, 2010a, p. 72):

- Estimating how much water and food is needed for emergency relief in a devastated city of three million people, and how it might be distributed.
- Planning a table tennis tournament for seven players at a club with four tables, where each player plays against every other player.
- Designing the layout of the stalls in a school fair so as to raise as much money as possible.
- Analyzing stopping distance for a car.
- Modeling savings account balance, bacterial colony growth, or investment growth.
- Engaging in critical path analysis, e.g., applied to turnaround of an aircraft at an airport.
- Analyzing risk in situations such as extreme sports, pandemics, and terrorism.
- Relating population statistics to individual predictions.

To be successful with modeling, students must develop their reasoning skills. They have to be critical problem solvers and must be able to ask questions while generating solutions. Children have natural problem-solving skills when they enter school. Unfortunately, a shallow procedural approach squashes this investigative ability. By using modeling within mathematics, students will once again become investigators and will discover that strategies used to solve one problem will also work for other problems. The Common Core modeling cycle is depicted in Exhibit 1.3.

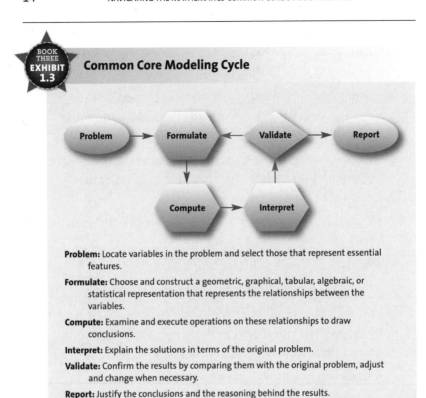

BOOK THREE EXHIBIT 1.3

Common Core Modeling Cycle

Problem: Locate variables in the problem and select those that represent essential features.

Formulate: Choose and construct a geometric, graphical, tabular, algebraic, or statistical representation that represents the relationships between the variables.

Compute: Examine and execute operations on these relationships to draw conclusions.

Interpret: Explain the solutions in terms of the original problem.

Validate: Confirm the results by comparing them with the original problem, adjust and change when necessary.

Report: Justify the conclusions and the reasoning behind the results.

Source: CCSSI, 2010a, p. 72.

Incorporating technology is a great way to inspire and motivate students. A natural "link" between modeling and the real world is the infusion of technology into the mathematics classroom. Technology is a vital part of the workplace, the global society, and students' lives. The mathematics classroom should prepare students for these environments by frequently, if not daily, incorporating technology into lessons and problem-solving structures. Technology is an invaluable tool in many applications. It can be used to:

- Quickly acquire results.
- Perform troublesome computations, allowing students time to deliberately think and problem solve.
- Provide opportunities for students to make new connections by displaying multiple representations of the same problem.
- Form and test conjectures by looking for patterns and relationships.
- Make adjustments because of incorrect conjectures.
- Generalize a solution.
- Collect data.
- Create graphs.
- Analyze data displays and best lines of fit.
- Create geometric constructions.
- Conduct research.

Besides being an engaging way to motivate students in the mathematics classroom, its use is required by the Common Core: "Strategic use of technology is expected in all work" (CCSSI, 2010b, p. 3). Technology, though, should not become a "crutch." It is vital that students have opportunities to develop both their conceptual and procedural understandings of math. Allowing students to have more than one type of technology to choose from and requiring them to justify their choice will help students understand the benefits and uses of technology. If students have a true conceptual understanding of the mathematical content being studied, then they will be able to test their predictions with or without the use of technology (NCTM, 2009, p. 14).

WHAT DOES IT MEAN TO BE MATHEMATICALLY COLLEGE- AND CAREER-READY?

In 2004, Achieve, along with the American Diploma Project, published *Ready or Not: Creating a High School Diploma That Counts.* The findings represented two years of research with the purpose of discovering why the American diploma was not preparing our students for post-secondary endeavors. Through this research, benchmarks were written in alignment with the expectations of colleges and workplaces across the country. This project challenged the nation's expectations of high school students and caused most states to begin looking at the rigor and expectations of their state standards as well as their high school exit exams. The CCSSI used this research when developing the Common Core State Standards, and considered how these standards can prepare students for a successful post-secondary experience whether in college or a career.

Today, the term "college- and career-ready" is an educational "buzzword." But what does it mean to be college- and career-ready? Achieve (2011) provides the following definition:

> "College and career readiness" refers to the content knowledge and skills high school graduates must possess in English and mathematics—including, but not limited to, reading, writing communications, teamwork, critical thinking and problem solving—to be

successful in any and all future endeavors. Of course, readiness for college and careers depends on more than English and mathematics knowledge; to be successful after high school, all graduates must possess the knowledge, habits and skills that can only come from a rigorous, rich, and well-rounded high school curriculum.

In essence, students who graduate with a high school diploma should be successful in post-secondary studies, regardless of enrollment in a four-year university, a community college, or a career training program. Entry into post-secondary studies should be accomplished without having to take remedial courses, which do not qualify for credit and sometimes not even financial assistance. Additionally, students who graduate with a high school diploma should be able to enter the workforce with the English and math skills necessary for successful performance in required post-secondary job training: vocational, technical, licenses, and so on. Note that "career," however, is defined differently than "job": "A career provides a family-sustaining wage and pathways to advancement and requires postsecondary training or education," but a job does not provide an assurance of expansion or flexibility (Achieve, 2011).

Are the requirements the same for both college readiness and career readiness? In today's society, the answer is yes. Students must be able to communicate, read, write, and solve complex problems in both post-secondary courses of study and in the workplace. Too many of our high school students graduate with a diploma and move on to college and/or the workplace only to find out they do not have the skills they need to be successful. In

Ready or Not: Creating a High School Diploma That Counts (Achieve, 2004, p. 3) the following statistics were published:

- Most high school graduates need remedial courses in college: 53 percent of students take at least one remedial English or math course, with the percentage of minority and poor students being much greater.

- Fewer than half of the students entering college ever graduate.

- More than 60 percent of employers rate high school graduates' grammar, writing, spelling, and basic math skills as "fair" or "poor." Employers have to spend millions of dollars a year providing remedial education for their employees.

- Many students do not take the more challenging courses offered in high school because they are not required for graduation.

- High school exams do not measure the skills needed for success in college and the workplace; instead they generally assess on an eighth- or ninth-grade level.

States are working on these issues, but unfortunately many high school students continue to graduate unprepared for life after high school.

The expectation from the Common Core is that *all* students will successfully study the standards for mathematical content and the standards for mathematical practice, which, in turn, will produce students who are college- and career-ready. For this to happen, though, states must require that all of the standards be taught. The expectation is that students will complete three years of mathematics encompassing all of the standards for mathematical content and practice, either through the traditional pathway of Algebra I, Geometry, and Algebra II, or an integrated pathway of Course I, II, and III (CCSSI, 2010a). Those states that currently require four years of mathematics need to ensure that the students meet or exceed the rigor suggested by the authors.

The rigor of the mathematics Common Core standards requires that districts, schools, and teachers be prepared to assist students throughout this demanding journey. "Watered down" courses should be stringently avoided. These courses do not inspire students to work harder and do not prepare students for the post-secondary requirements awaiting them. High expectations are key to the success of all students. For those students who struggle or fall behind in mathematics, schools should provide support in addition to "response to intervention" strategies by looking at the structure of the school day. To provide more time for in-depth intervention, schools should consider offering additional math support classes within the instructional day, before- or after-school tutoring, block classes, and summer school. The primary goal is to ensure that *all* students achieve *all* standards (CCSSI, 2010b, pp. 4–5).

> *Now is the accepted time, not tomorrow, not some more convenient season. It is today that our best work can be done and not some future day or future year. It is today that we fit ourselves for the greater usefulness of tomorrow. Today is the seed time, now are the hours of work, and tomorrow comes the harvest and the playtime.*
>
> —W. E. B. Du Bois

SUMMARY

The Common Core State Standards for Mathematics require that high school math instruction focus on helping students develop a true understanding of mathematics, not just the ability to perform mathematical procedures. The Common Core also insists that *all* students demonstrate mastery of rigorous math standards, not just those planning careers in science, technology, engineering, and mathematics.

The high school Common Core mathematics standards are organized into six conceptual categories: number and quantity, algebra, functions, geometry, statistics and probability, and modeling. The modeling standards are incorporated throughout the other five categories, indicated by a star symbol ($\star$). Each category contains an overview, an introduction, a list of eight standards for mathematical practice, and the content standards.

The content standards are grouped into domains (broad themes) and clusters (groups of similar standards). The high school standards are the college- and career-readiness standards and are to be achieved by all students. Advanced course work standards are included as well and are indicated by a plus symbol ($+$).

Appendix A of the Common Core State Standards for Mathematics contains model course pathways. These pathways are not intended to be directives or to endorse a particular curriculum or sequence of instruction, but rather to be examples for schools to use when creating their own mathematics curricula. The example pathways provided in Appendix A are: traditional, integrated, "compacted" traditional, and "compacted" integrated.

The Common Core documents stress the importance of modeling in the mathematics classroom and depict modeling as essential to student engagement and learning. The term "modeling" is used not to describe showing students how to conduct a procedure, but rather how to link mathematics to real-world situations in a meaningful way. Incorporation of technology into the classroom is also expected.

The Common Core high school mathematics standards require students to persevere through their mathematics studies, reason mathematically, and practice connecting mathematical ways of thinking to real-world applications and the challenges that await them after graduation. The high school standards are a rigorous set of standards that prepare students for post-secondary success by requiring them to cultivate an understanding and ability to apply mathematics to unique situations, as college students and employees regularly do (CCSSI, 2010c).

The crisis that is upon us does not have to overcome us. We are living in a very exciting time in the history of American education, and by deeply embedding the Common Core's standards for mathematical practice into the standards for mathematical content, we will successfully prepare *all* high school students for the careers of the 21st century.

> *You are not here merely to make a living. You are here to enable the world to live more amply, with greater vision, and with a finer spirit of hope and achievement. You are here to enrich the world, and you impoverish yourself if you forget this errand.*
>
> —Woodrow Wilson

References

Achieve. (2004). *Ready or not: Creating a high school diploma that counts.* Retrieved from www.achieve.org/ReadyorNot

Achieve. (retrieved in 2011). *What is college- and career-ready?* Retrieved from www.achieve.org/files/CollegeandCareerReady.pdf

Common Core State Standards Initiative (CCSSI). (2010a, June). *Common Core State Standards for mathematics* (PDF document). Retrieved from www.corestandards.org/assets/CCSSI_Math %20Standards.pdf

Common Core State Standards Initiative (CCSSI). (2010b, June). *Common Core State Standards for mathematics: Appendix A* (PDF document). Retrieved from www.corestandards.org/assets/CCSSI _Mathematics_Appendix_A.pdf

Common Core State Standards Initiative (CCSSI). (2010c, June). *Key points in mathematics.* Retrieved from www.corestandards.org/ about-the-standards/key-points-in-mathematics

Leinwand, S. (2010, Oct. 7). Presentation, American Institutes for Research, at NCTM Regional Conference, Denver.

National Council of Teachers of Mathematics (NCTM). (2009). *Focus in high school mathematics: Reasoning and sense making.* Reston, VA: NCTM.

National Research Council. (2001). *Adding it up: Helping children learn mathematics.* J. Kilpatrick, J. Swafford, & B. Findell (Eds.). Mathematics Learning Study Committee, Center for Education, Division of Behavioral and Social Sciences Education. Washington, DC: National Academies Press.

Reys, B. J., Dingman, S., Nevels, N., & Teuscher, D. (2007). *High school mathematics: State-level curriculum standards and graduation requirements.* Retrieved from www.mathcurriculumcenter.org/ PDFS/HSreport.pdf

How the K–8 Learning Progressions Influence Planning for Instruction and Assessment

Jan Christinson

In the introduction to *Learning Progressions Frameworks Designed for Use with the Common Core State Standards in Mathematics K–12*, Project Director Karin K. Hess presents an effective summary of researchers' attempts to define learning progressions (2010, p. 2):

> For example, Wilson and Bertenthal (2005) define in terms of "descriptions of the successively more sophisticated ways of thinking about an idea that follow one another as students learn"; while Masters and Forster (1996) see them as "a picture of the path students typically follow as they learn ... a description of skills, understandings, and knowledge in the sequence in which they typically develop." Duschl, Schweingruber, and Shouse (2007) describe learning progressions as "anchored on one end by what is known about the concepts and reasoning of students entering school ... [for which] there now is a very ex-

tensive research base." At the other end of the learning continuum are "societal expectations (values)" about what society wants students to know and be able to do in the given content area. Learning progressions propose the intermediate understandings between these anchor points that are "reasonably coherent networks of ideas and practices ... that contribute to building a more mature understanding." (Hess, 2008)

In the introduction to the Common Core State Standards for Mathematics, the authors discuss learning progressions within the description of "How to read the grade level standards" (CCSSI, 2010, p.5):

Ideally then, each standard in this document might have been phrased in the form, "Students who already know ... should next come to learn. ..." But at present this approach is unrealistic—not least because existing education research cannot specify all such learning pathways. Of necessity, therefore, grade placements for specific topics have been made on the basis of state and international comparisons and the collective professional judgment of educators, researchers and mathematicians. One promise of common state standards is that over time they will allow research on learning progressions to inform and improve the design of standards to a much greater extent than is possible today.

In this chapter, learning progressions for several key topics in mathematics are examined by looking at how the Common Core State Standards developed understanding for those topics across the grades from kindergarten through grade 8. This vertical examination of the standards, centered on an individual topic, gives insight into how the authors of the Common Core believe a concept is learned over time, and about their philosophy of how students learn mathematics effectively. Knowledge of learning progressions can benefit the process of curriculum design, improve diagnosis of student misconceptions, inform intervention processes for students struggling in mathematics, and ultimately improve teacher knowledge of how students learn mathematics.

Each learning progression is presented in chart form to facilitate examination of the steps in the learning process from kindergarten to grade 8. The charts contain phrases and concepts from the Common Core standards for each grade that pertain to the named topic. (Note that some standards are listed several times to highlight their component parts.) Each learning progression chart is followed by a summary that provides an overview of the learning progression and in some instances key points to consider.

Learning Progressions—Charts and Summaries

Learning Progression for Measurement and Data—Represent and Interpret Data

Grades K–2	Grades 3–5	Grades 6–8 (Statistics)
Kindergarten **K.MD.3**—Classify objects into given categories, count number of objects in a category, sort categories by count **Grade 1** **1.MD.4**—Represent and interpret data **1.MD.4**—Ask and answer: "How many in each category?" **1.MD.4**—Ask and answer: "How many more or less in one category?" **Grade 2** **2.MD.9,10**—Represent and interpret data **2.MD.9**—Generate measurement data by measuring length to nearest whole unit, show data on line plot **2.MD.10**—Draw picture graph and bar graph to represent data set up to four categories **2.MD.10**—Solve compare problems using data on graph	**Grade 3** **3.MD.3,4**—Represent and interpret data **3.MD.3**—Draw a scaled picture graph, scaled bar graph with several categories **3.MD.3**—Solve how many more, how many less problems using bar graph **3.MD.4**—Generate measurement data using a ruler marked with halves and fourths of a unit. Put data on line plot **Grade 4** **4.MD.4**—Make a line plot to display data set of measurements in fractions of a unit (1/2, 1/4, 1/8) **4.MD.4**—Solve problems using data involving addition and subtraction of fractions by using information presented in line plots **Grade 5** **5.MD.2**—Represent and interpret data **5.MD.2**—Use operations on fractions for this grade to solve problems	**Grade 6** **6.SP.1,2,3**—Develop understanding of statistical variability **6.SP.2**—Understand that a set of data collected to answer a statistical question has a distribution which can be described by its center, spread, and overall shape **6.SP.5b,c**—Summarize and describe distributions using description of the attribute being investigated, measures of center, overall pattern, and striking deviations from the pattern **Grade 7** **7.SP.1,2**—Use random sampling to draw inferences about a population **7.SP.3,4**—Draw informal comparative inferences about two populations using measures of center **Grade 8** **8.SP.1**—Construct and interpret scatter plots for bivariate measurement data to investigate patterns of association between two quantities **8.SP.3**—Use slope and intercept to solve problems involving bivariate measurement data **8.SP.4**—Construct and interpret a two-way table summarizing data on two categorical variables collected from the same subjects

Summary

The learning progression for the domain "Measurement and Data—Represent and
Interpret Data" begins with kindergarten and grade 1 students classifying objects
in categories, counting the objects in the categories, and then performing
comparisons between categories. Grade 2, grade 3, and grade 4 students generate
data by measuring length and showing data on a line plot. In grade 3 through
grade 5, the measurement data is connected to fraction development. Grade 6
students begin to think statistically and learn about different measures of the
center of the data and look at the overall shape of the data. Grade 7 students move
from single data distributions to comparing two data distributions and addressing
differences between populations. Grade 8 students use scatter plots to look at
patterns of association between two quantities and they interpret data within the
context of their work with linear equations. There is an emphasis across the grades
on interpretation of the display of data that has been generated. Notice that the
use of different measures of central tendency is introduced in grade 6 when
students begin thinking statistically, as opposed to the typical procedural approach
to mean, median, and mode that often happens in grade 4.

Learning Progression for Geometry—Shapes

Grades K–2	Grades 3–5	Grades 6–8
Kindergarten	**Grade 3**	**Grade 6**
K.G.1—Identify and describe shapes	**3.G.1,2**—Reason with shapes and their attributes	**6.G.3**—Draw polygons in the coordinate plane using coordinates; Use coordinates to find length
K.G.4—Analyze, compare, create, compose shapes	**3.G.1**—Recognize that shapes in different categories may share attributes	**6.G.4**—Represent three-dimensional figures using nets made up of rectangles and triangles; Use nets to find surface area
Grade 1	**3.G.2**—Relate fraction work to shapes	
1.G.1,2,3—Reason with shapes and their attributes	**Grade 4**	**Grade 7**
1.G.1—Build and draw shapes with defining attributes	**4.G.2**—Classify two-dimensional figures using parallel and perpendicular lines and angles	**7.G.1,2,3**—Draw, construct, describe geometric figures and describe relationships between them
1.G.2—Compose two- or three-dimensional shapes to create a composite shape	**4.G.3**—Recognize lines of symmetry; Identify figures with line symmetry	**7.G.4,5,6**—Solve problems involving scale drawings of geometric figures
1.G.3—Partition circles and rectangles into two and four equal shares	**Grade 5**	**Grade 8**
Grade 2	**5.G.2**—Graph points on the coordinate plane in the first quadrant	**8.G.2**—Understand congruence and similarity in terms of properties of rotations, reflections, and translations
2.G.1,2,3—Reason with shapes and their attributes	**5.G.3,4**—Classify two-dimensional figures into categories based on properties	
2.G.1—Draw shapes with specified attributes (angles, faces)		
2.G.2—Partition rectangles to find the number of square units within the rectangle by counting		
2.G.3—Partition circles and rectangles to find halves and thirds		

Summary

In kindergarten through grade 3, students are learning to reason with and construct shapes based on the attributes of the shapes. Students in grade 1 through grade 3 work with partitioning shapes, which is connected to the development of part-whole relationships. This becomes the basis for understanding fractions. Grade 2 students build the foundation for understanding area, volume, congruence, similarity, and symmetry through the construction of shapes and the partitioning of shapes. Grade 3 students increase their awareness of the classification process based on attributes. Classification of two-dimensional shapes in grade 4 is based on parallel and perpendicular lines, which leads students to the use of angles and lines of symmetry in their analysis of polygons. Grade 5 students further refine the classification process of two-dimensional figures by generalizing attributes of a category to subcategories of that category. Also, they are introduced to the coordinate plane built from two perpendicular lines. Grade 6 students decompose three-dimensional shapes into nets to find surface area. They prepare for scale drawing work by finding lengths of sides of polygons on the coordinate plane. Students in grade 7 prepare for the concepts of congruence and similarity by constructing and describing geometric figures and discussing the relationships between them. In grade 8, students' previous work with attributes and properties of figures culminates in the use of similarity and congruence to describe and analyze two-dimensional figures.

The Common Core emphasizes reasoning with attributes and properties of figures across the grades as opposed to only identifying figures, which typically is a vocabulary exercise.

Learning Progression for Problem Solving

Grades K–2	Grades 3–4	Grades 5–8
Kindergarten **K.OA.2**—Solve addition and subtraction word problems within 10 using objects or drawings to represent the problem **Grade 1** **1.OA.1**—Use addition and subtraction within 20 to solve word problems involving situations of adding to, taking from, putting together, taking apart, and comparing **Grade 2** **2.OA.1**—Use addition and subtraction within 100 to solve one- and two-step word problems involving situations of adding to, taking from, putting together, taking apart, and comparing with unknowns in all positions **2.MD.5**—Use addition and subtraction within 100 to solve word problems involving lengths given in the same unit **2.MD.8**—Solve word problems involving dollar bills, quarters, dimes, nickels, and pennies.	**Grade 3** **3.OA.3**—Use multiplication and division within 100 to solve word problems in situations involving equal groups, arrays, and measurement quantities **3.OA.8**—Solve two-step problems using the four operations **3.MD.1,2**—Solve problems involving measurement and estimation of intervals of time, liquid volumes, and masses of objects **3.MD.8**—Solve real-world and mathematical problems involving perimeters of polygons **Grade 4** **4.OA.3**—Use the four operations with whole numbers to solve problems, including problems in which remainders must be interpreted **4.NF.3d**—Solve word problems involving addition and subtraction of fractions referring to the same whole and having like denominators **4.NF.4c**—Solve word problems involving multiplication of a fraction by a whole number **4.MD.2**—Use the four operations to solve word problems involving distances, intervals of time, liquid volumes, masses of objects, and money **4.MD.3**—Apply the area and perimeter formulas for rectangles in real-world and mathematical problems	**Grade 5** **5.NF.2,6**—Solve word problems involving addition and subtraction of fractions, and multiplication of fractions and mixed numbers **5.MD.5**—Solve real-world problems involving volume **Grade 6** **6.RP.3**—Use ratio and rate reasoning to solve real-world and mathematical problems **6.NS.8**—Solve real-world and mathematical problems by graphing points in all four quadrants of the coordinate plane **6.EE.7**—Solve real-world problems and mathematical problems by writing and solving equations of the form $x + p = q$ and $px = q$ for cases in which p, q, and x are all nonnegative rational numbers **Grade 7** **7.RP.1,2,3**—Analyze proportional relationships and use them to solve real-world and mathematical problems **7.NS.3**—Solve real-world and mathematical problems involving the four operations with rational numbers **7.EE.3,4**—Solve real-life and mathematical problems using numerical and algebraic expressions and equations **Grade 8** **8.EE.8c**—Solve real-world and mathematical problems leading to two linear equations in two variables

Summary

Problem solving is emphasized in all grades in the Common Core State Standards. In the standards for mathematical practice, the first practice listed is "make sense of problems and persevere in solving them." An excellent description of the problem-solving process that mathematically proficient students follow is provided. Besides listing problem solving as a key expertise to develop in students, the Common Core State Standards are specific in each grade as to where problem solving should take place. Kindergarten and grade 1 students solve word problems with numbers from 1–20. Students in grade 2 work on problems that involve one or two steps and the contexts of money and length. Grade 3 students solve problems with equal groups, the four operations, measurement concepts, time, money, mass, and perimeter. Students in grade 4 continue problem solving within the four operations, then move on to do problem solving with interpretation of remainders in division, fractions, area, and perimeter. Grade 5 students solve problems using fraction concepts and volume. Problem solving in the middle grades is focused on the use of proportional reasoning. Grade 6 students solve problems using ratio and rate, the coordinate plane, and simple equations. In grade 7, students use proportional relationships to solve problems involving the four operations with rational numbers. They also use algebraic expressions and equations to solve problems. In grade 8, students solve problems that lead to the use of two linear equations with two variables.

In grades 3 through 8, there is an emphasis on applying the problem-solving work that students do to real-world contexts.

Learning Progression for Multiplication and Division

Grade 2	Grades 3–4	Grades 5–7
Grade 2	**Grade 3**	**Grade 5**
2.OA.3,4—Work with equal groups of objects to gain foundations for multiplication	**3.OA.1**—Interpret products of whole numbers	**5.NBT.5**—Fluently multiply multi-digit whole numbers using the standard algorithm
2.OA.3—Determine whether a group of objects has an odd or even number of members	**3.OA.2**—Interpret whole-number quotients of whole numbers	**5.NBT.6**—Find whole-number quotients of whole numbers with up to four-digit dividends and two-digit divisors
2.OA.4—Use addition to find the total number of objects arranged in rectangular arrays with up to 5 rows and up to 5 columns	**3.OA.3**—Use multiplication and division within 100 to solve word problems	**5.NBT.7**—Add, subtract, multiply, and divide decimals to hundredths using models, drawings, place value and the properties of operations
	3.OA.5—Apply properties of operations as strategies to multiply and divide	
	3.OA.6—Understand division as an unknown-factor problem	**Grade 6**
	3.OA.7—Fluently multiply and divide within 100	**6.NS.2**—Fluently divide multi-digit numbers using the standard algorithm
	3.NBT.3—Multiply one-digit whole numbers by multiples of 10 in the range 10–90 using strategies based on place value and properties of operations	**6.NS.3**—Fluently add, subtract, multiply, and divide multi-digit decimals using the standard algorithm for each operation
		6.NS.4—Find common factors and multiples
	Grade 4	
	4.OA.1—Interpret a multiplication equation as a comparison	**Grade 7**
	4.OA.4—Gain familiarity with factors and multiples	**7.NS.2**—Apply and extend previous understandings of multiplication and division and of fractions to multiply and divide rational numbers
	4.NBT.5—Multiply a whole number of up to four digits by a one-digit whole number and multiply two two-digit numbers using strategies based on place value and properties of operations	
	4.NBT.6—Find whole-number quotients and remainders with up to four-digit dividends and one-digit divisors using strategies based on place value and properties of operations	

Summary

This learning progression develops the concepts of multiplication and division together over grades 3, 4, 5, and 6, and then has students apply their understanding to operations with rational numbers in grade 7. The foundation for multiplication is developed in grade 2 through work with equal groups and rectangular arrays. Grade 3 students begin with interpreting products and quotients of whole numbers, then use their understanding to solve problems with numbers within 100. Then students apply properties of operations (number sense) to multiply and divide, finally moving to fluency with multiplying and dividing within 100. To support fluency, students are expected to know from memory all products of two one-digit numbers by the end of grade 3. Grade 4 students continue their work with multiplication and division by using strategies based on place value and number properties to perform operations with multi-digit whole numbers. To further their understanding of multiplication and division, grade 4 students learn about factors and multiples. Grade 5 students develop fluency with multi-digit multiplication using the standard algorithm and extend their work with multi-digit division to include two-digit divisors. Students in grade 5 also apply their understanding of the four operations with whole numbers to decimals to the hundredths place. In grade 6, students fluently divide multi-digit numbers using the standard algorithm, and they involve common factors and multiples in their computations with multi-digit numbers. Grade 7 students apply and extend the previous understanding of multiplication and division with whole numbers to rational numbers.

The Common Core State Standards have increased the amount and level of understanding that needs to take place in grade 3. This learning progression takes the approach of developing understanding of the concept, then developing connection to other concepts, and then developing fluency with a standard algorithm. Specifically, students work with equal groups, interpret products and quotients, use place value and properties of operations to find strategies to solve problems, and then develop fluency with a standard algorithm. This process happens over several grade levels.

Learning Progression for Basic Math Facts

Grades K–2	Grades 3–5	Grade 6
Kindergarten **K.OA.5**—Fluently add and subtract within 5 **Grade 1** **1.OA.6**—Add and subtract within 20, demonstrating fluency for addition and subtraction within 10 **Grade 2** **2.OA.2**—Fluently add and subtract within 20 using mental strategies **2.OA.2**—By the end of grade 2, know from memory all sums of two one-digit numbers	**Grade 3** **3.OA.7**—By the end of grade 3, know from memory all products of two one-digit numbers **Grade 4** **4.NBT.4**—Fluently add and subtract multi-digit whole numbers using the standard algorithm **Grade 5** **5.NBT.5**—Fluently multiply multi-digit whole numbers using the standard algorithm	**Grade 6** **6.NS.2**—Fluently divide multi-digit numbers using the standard algorithm

Summary

There is a major emphasis in the early grades on the development of number concepts in the Common Core State Standards. The introduction page in the Common Core document for each grade level suggests areas for focus of instructional time. The introduction pages for kindergarten to grade 4 all contain a focus topic that supports the development of fluency with basic operations. The emphasis in the Common Core seems to be fluency with operations as opposed to just memorization of basic number facts or memorization of procedural steps. The development of fluency within an operation is based on understanding of the operation, finding strategies from other number properties that have been learned, and then development of fluency with that operation. Considering the expectation of fluency with traditional algorithms, it is interesting to look at the expectations for memorization of basic number facts within the standards. Kindergarten students are asked to show fluency with addition and subtraction within 5. Grade 1 students are expected to extend that fluency to numbers within 10. Grade 2 students move from fluency with addition and subtraction within 20 to knowing from memory all sums of two one-digit numbers. By the end of grade 3, students are expected to know from memory all products of two one-digit numbers. Notice that in grade 2 subtraction basic facts are not mentioned, and in grade 3 division basic facts are not mentioned. The Common Core standards are taking a number sense approach; students will use addition to access subtraction facts, and they will use multiplication to access division facts. Grades 4, 5, and 6 continue the pattern of expecting fluency with operations with multi-digit numbers using standard algorithms. This expectation of fluency with standard algorithms is very dependent upon fluency with basic number facts.

Learning Progression for Fractions

Grades K–3	Grades 4–5	Grades 6–8
Kindergarten **K.G.6**—Compose simple shapes to form larger shapes **Grade 1** **1.G.3**—Partition circles and rectangles into two and four equal shares; describe the shares using the words halves, fourths, and quarters **Grade 2** **2.G.3**—Partition circles and rectangles into two, three, or four equal shares; describe the shares using the words halves, thirds, fourths **Grade 3** **3.NF.1**—Develop understanding of fractions as numbers **3.NF.2**—Understand a fraction as a number on the number line **3.NF.3**—Explain equivalence of fractions in special cases and compare fractions by reasoning about their size	**Grade 4** **4.NF.1,2**—Extend understanding of fraction equivalence and ordering **4.NF.3a**—Understand addition and subtraction of fractions as joining and separating parts referring to the same whole **4.NF.3c**—Add and subtract mixed numbers with like denominators **4.NF.4**—Apply and extend previous understandings of multiplication to multiply a fraction by a whole number **4.NF.5,6,7**—Understand decimal notation for fractions and compare decimal fractions **Grade 5** **5.NF.1**—Use equivalent fractions as a strategy to add and subtract fractions **5.NF.2**—Use benchmark fractions and number sense of fractions to estimate mentally and assess reasonableness of answers **5.NF.4**—Apply and extend previous understandings of multiplication to multiply a fraction or whole number by a fraction **5.NF.7**—Apply and extend previous understandings of division to divide unit fractions by whole numbers and whole numbers by unit fractions	**Grade 6** **6.NS.1**—Apply and extend previous understandings of multiplication and division to divide fractions by fractions **Grade 7** **7.NS.1**—Apply and extend previous understandings of operations with fractions to add, subtract, multiply, and divide rational numbers **Grade 8** **8.EE.7b**—Solve linear equations with rational number coefficients

Summary

The learning progression for fractions begins with kindergarten students composing shapes and gaining experience with part-whole relationships. Students in grade 1 compose and decompose plane or solid figures to gain more understanding of part-whole relationships. Grade 2 students continue work decomposing and combining shapes to make other shapes. Students partition circles and rectangles into two, three, and four equal pieces and then use fractional words to describe each piece. Grade 3 students develop an understanding of fractions through the use of unit fractions and also begin work with the relative size of fractions. Grade 4 students extend understanding of fraction equivalence through the use of models and begin work with operations with fractions, including multiplying a fraction by a whole number. By grade 5, students are expected to develop fluency with addition and subtraction of fractions and develop understanding of multiplying a fraction or whole number by a fraction. Students also apply previous understanding of division to divide unit fractions by whole numbers and whole numbers by fractions. Grade 6 students extend their understanding of fractions to interpret and compute quotients of fractions and solve problems involving division of fractions by fractions. In grade 7, students apply their understanding of operations with fractions to operations with rational numbers.

The Common Core State Standards emphasize understanding of fraction concepts and development of that understanding over several grade levels. The Common Core assumes that by the end of sixth grade, students are fluent with operations related to fractions.

Learning Progression for Algebraic Thinking/Expressions and Equations

Grades K–2	Grades 3–5	Grades 6–8
Kindergarten **K.OA.3**—Decompose numbers less than or equal to 10 into pairs in more than one way **K.OA.4**—For any number from 1 to 9, find the number that makes 10 when added to the given number **Grade 1** **1.OA.7**—Understand the meaning of the equal sign, and determine if equations involving addition and subtraction are true or false **1.OA.8**—Determine the unknown whole number in an addition or subtraction equation relating three whole numbers **Grade 2** **2.OA.1**—Use addition and subtraction within 100 to solve one- and two-step word problems involving situations of adding to, taking from, putting together, taking apart, and comparing with unknowns in all positions	**Grade 3** **3.OA.4**—Determine the unknown whole number in a multiplication or division equation relating three whole numbers **3.OA.8**—Solve two-step word problems using four operations. Represent these problems using equations with a letter standing for the unknown quantity **Grade 4** **4.OA.2**—Multiply or divide to solve word problems involving multiplicative comparison by using equations with a symbol for the unknown number **4.OA.5**—Generate a number pattern or shape pattern that follows a given rule **Grade 5** **5.OA.3**—Analyze patterns and relationships **5.OA.3**—Identify apparent relationships between corresponding terms **5.OA.3**—Form ordered pairs from pattern and graph ordered pairs on coordinate plane **5.OA.2**—Write simple expressions that record calculations with numbers	**Grade 6** **6.EE.1,2,3,4**—Apply and extend previous understandings of arithmetic to algebraic expressions **6.EE.5,6,7,8**—Reason about and solve one-variable equations and inequalities **6.EE.9**—Represent and analyze quantitative relationships between dependent and independent variables **Grade 7** **7.EE.1,2**—Use properties of operations to generate equivalent expressions **7.EE.4**—Use variables to represent quantities in a real-world or mathematical problem, and construct simple equations and inequalities to solve problems by reasoning about the quantities **7.EE.4a**—Solve two-step equations **Grade 8** **8.EE.5,6**—Understand the connections between proportional relationships, lines, and linear equations **8.EE.7,8**—Analyze and solve linear equations and pairs of simultaneous linear equations

Summary

In *Elementary and Middle School Mathematics—Teaching Developmentally*, John Van de Walle discusses algebraic thinking: "Algebraic thinking involves forming generalizations from experiences with number and computation, formalizing these ideas with the use of a meaningful symbol system, and exploring the concepts of pattern and functions" (2007, p. 259).

He continues with a recommendation for curriculum: "It is a separate strand of the curriculum but should also be embedded in all areas of mathematics. There is general agreement that we must begin the development of these forms of thinking from the very beginning of school so that students will learn to think productively with the powerful ideas of mathematics—so that they can think mathematically" (Van de Walle, 2007, p. 260).

This learning progression demonstrates how the Common Core State Standards have effectively created expectations for algebraic thinking from kindergarten to grade 8.

Kindergarten students work with adding and subtracting quantities, and they represent their work with drawings and equations. Grade 1 students learn about the meaning of the equal sign (a critical understanding in algebraic reasoning), and they work with addition and subtraction equations that contain an unknown. Students in grade 2 solve one- and two-step word problems with addition and subtraction, and represent their work with drawings and equations that contain a symbol for the unknown quantity. Grade 3 students continue the same type of work with multiplication and division word problems. In grade 4, students solve word problems using the four operations and represent these problems with equations that contain a letter for the unknown quantity. They also begin exploring the idea of function by generating a pattern that follows a given rule. Grade 5 students gain more experience with functional reasoning by generating two patterns using two rules and graphing the results on the coordinate plane. They also write simple expressions that record their calculations with numbers. In grade 6, the title for this domain of the Common Core standards is changed to "Expressions and Equations," signifying that students will be involved in the more formal process of manipulating and solving linear equations. Grade 6 students solve one-step equations and inequalities. Grade 7 students solve one- and two-step equations and inequalities with positive and negative rational numbers. In grade 8, students extend their work with equations to include the use of the distributive property, combining like terms, slope, and solving simultaneous equations.

The Common Core standards connect algebraic thinking and work with expressions and equations to problem-solving situations across all the grade levels from kindergarten to grade 8 and effectively link prior work with arithmetic to algebraic expressions. From this learning progression, it is apparent that the Common Core promotes algebraic reasoning and thinking, as opposed to the more typical system of symbol manipulation that is presented as algebra.

IMPLICATIONS OF THE LEARNING PROGRESSIONS FOR TEACHERS AND ADMINISTRATORS

An examination of the learning progressions developed within the Common Core State Standards reveals that the standards are promoting that students understand the math concepts they are learning, become fluent with the operations attached to those concepts, and apply their understanding to problem-solving situations on a regular basis. This approach to teaching mathematics, and the learning philosophy that supports such an approach, has many implications for teachers and administrators. There are many questions for teachers and administrators to consider as they move toward implementation of the Common Core.

Instructional Practice

- Does the current instructional model for mathematics in your school support teaching for understanding?

- Is the current instructional model for mathematics balanced in terms of building number sense, computational fluency, and conceptual understanding, and providing for application of the mathematical concepts students are learning (problem solving)?

- Is there a math fact program in place that includes a strong instructional component and an assessment component?

- How will the current textbook series be used? Does the series match the direction and philosophy of the Common Core State Standards? How will the textbook be used as a resource in light of the changes in expectations in the Common Core?

- Is the primary (K–2) instructional program focused on number sense development?

- Is there a systematic review process in place based on error analysis, feedback, and student reflection that will support development of fluency with the four operations?

- Is there a problem-solving program in place in grades K–12?

Teacher Content Knowledge

- Do teachers feel prepared to teach math conceptually (with understanding)?

- Is there a support process for teachers available to build more capacity to teach conceptually?

- Is there a process to involve teachers in becoming aware of the student learning expectations in the Common Core?

- Are teachers aware of how a student develops understanding of a concept across several grade levels, and is this information used in planning lessons?

- Are teachers aware of the origins of student misconceptions pertaining to a concept?

- Are teachers designing units of study around essential ideas in collaborative teams (an excellent method to build teacher content knowledge in a supportive environment)?

Classroom Environment
(How students learn mathematics)

- Is the math classroom environment conducive to the learning of mathematics? Are students engaged in conversation, interaction, and metacognitive practices focused on the mathematics they are learning?

- Is there a balance of teacher talk and student talk during instruction?

- Are the standards for mathematical practice that are part of the Common Core State Standards promoted in the classroom? (The standards for mathematical practice are: make sense of problems and persevere in solving them; reason abstractly and quantitatively; construct viable arguments and critique the reasoning of others; model with mathematics; use appropriate tools strategically; attend to precision; look for and make structure; look for and express regularity in repeated reasoning.)

- Are student mistakes seen as opportunities to learn?

Teacher Support/School-Level Concerns

- Do teachers operate in collaborative teams?

- Is there a process in the school to facilitate discussion across grade levels to examine learning progressions for math concepts?

- Is there a process to consider learning progressions in the curriculum design process?

• How will units of study be designed and sequenced based on the vertical learning progressions presented in the Common Core?

SUMMARY

The learning progressions in the Common Core State Standards for Mathematics make it clear that certain components are essential to an effective mathematics instructional model and assessment model.

An effective Common Core mathematics instructional model should include:

• Teaching for understanding.

• Regular problem solving.

• An emphasis on number sense development in grades K–2.

• An instructional component to math fact fluency development.

• A balanced instructional approach that includes development of computational strength, application of the mathematics, and understanding of the mathematics.

An effective Common Core mathematics assessment model should include:

• Assessment tools that inform the teacher about student understanding of key concepts.

• Various forms of assessment to provide evidence of student misconception.

- The consistent use of student mistakes to inform instruction.

- Common assessments across a grade level to allow for collaborative discussion of student understanding.

- Development of student metacognitive skills to increase quality of evidence gathered from assessment tools.

- Assessments that provide timely and specific feedback to students.

References

Common Core State Standards Initiative (CCSSI). (2010, June). *Common Core State Standards for mathematics* (PDF document). Retrieved from www.corestandards.org/assets/CCSSI_Math %20Standards.pdf

Duschl, R., Schweingruber, H., & Shouse, A. (2007). *Taking science to school: Learning and teaching science in grades K–8.* Board on Science Education. Washington, DC: National Academies Press.

Hess, K. (2008). *Developing and using learning progressions as a schema for measuring progress.* Retrieved from www.nciea.org/publications/ CCSSO2_KH08.pdf

Hess, K. (2010, December). *Learning progressions frameworks designed for use with the Common Core State Standards in mathematics K–12.* National Alternate Assessment Center at the University of Kentucky. Retrieved from www.nciea.org/publications/ Math_LPF_KH11.pdf

Masters, G., & Forster, M. (1996). *Progress maps* (part of the *Assessment resource kit*). Melbourne, Australia: The Australian Council for Educational Research.

Van de Walle, J. (2007). *Elementary and middle school mathematics— Teaching developmentally* (6th ed.). Boston, MA: Pearson.

Wilson, M., & Bertenthal, M. (Eds.). (2005). *Systems for state science assessment.* Board on Testing and Assessment, Center for Education, National Research Council of the National Academies. Washington, DC: National Academies Press.

Integrating the Standards for Mathematical Practice with the Standards for Mathematical Content

Jan Christinson

*Believe in kids! Allow them to think, to struggle,
and to reason with new ideas as together you find
the excitement that happens when mathematics
makes sense.*

—John Van de Walle (2007, p. xvii)

There has been controversy surrounding mathematics education in the United States for decades, if not longer. Educators and researchers involved in writing curriculum, developing textbooks, or writing state standards have had to wrestle with fundamental questions about how students learn mathematics and how mathematics should be taught. Many decisions about math instruction have been based on tradition or very little actual research information. Before writing the Common Core State Standards for Mathematics, the authors had to examine research and come to agreement as to how they think students learn mathematics and what impact that determination has on classroom practices. The Common Core's standards for mathematical practice were a result of that process. The committee relied upon work by the National Council of Teachers of Mathematics in *Principles and Standards for School Mathematics* (2000) and the National Research Council's *Adding It Up* (2001) to produce the standards for mathematical practice.

> These practices rest on important "processes and proficiencies" with longstanding importance in mathematics education. The first of these are the NCTM process standards of problem solving, reasoning and proof, communication, representation, and connections. The second are the strands of mathematical proficiency specified in the National Research Council's report *Adding It Up*: adaptive reasoning, strategic competence, conceptual understanding (comprehension of mathematical concepts, operations and relations), procedural fluency (skill in carrying out procedures flexibly, accurately, efficiently, and appropriately), and productive disposition (habitual inclination to see mathematics as sensible, useful, and worthwhile, coupled with a belief in diligence and one's own efficacy). (CCSSI, 2010, p. 6)

Following are some of the essential ideas from research that influenced the development of the Common Core's standards for mathematical practice:

> • Mathematical proficiency has five strands: conceptual understanding, procedural fluency, strategic competence, adaptive reasoning, and productive disposition. The strands are interwoven and interdependent.

- The teaching and learning of mathematics is the product of interactions among the teacher, the students, and the mathematics.

- The quality of instruction is a function of the teacher's knowledge and use of mathematical content, the teacher's attention to and handling of students, and the student's engagement in and use of mathematical tasks.

- Opportunity to learn is widely considered the single most important predictor of student achievement.

- Students need to believe that what they are learning in mathematics is worth learning.

- Educators can motivate students to value learning mathematics by emphasizing topics they find interesting and tasks they find enjoyable.

- Students are motivated to learn mathematics by responding actively rather than merely listening, by having opportunities to interact with their peers, by being provided with situations that invite thought (such as being asked divergent questions), and by participating in activities with game-like features, such as puzzles and brainteasers.

- Creating a classroom that functions as a community of learners involves four important ideas from *Adding It Up* (National Research Council, 2001, p. 344):

  1. All ideas and methods are valued. Ideas expressed by any student warrant respect and response and have potential to contribute to everyone's learning.

2. Students have autonomy in choosing and sharing their methods of solving problems. They respect the methods used by others. They are given freedom to explore alternatives and to share their thinking with the rest of the class.

3. There is appreciation of the value of mistakes as sites of learning for everyone. Mistakes are used as opportunities to examine reasoning and to deepen everyone's analysis.

4. There is recognition that the authority for whether something is both correct and sensible lies in the logic and structure of the subject rather than the status of the teacher or the popularity of the person making the argument.

• Teachers must make judgments about when to tell, when to question, and when to correct. They must decide when to guide with prompting and when to let students grapple with a mathematical issue.

MATHEMATICAL PRACTICE STANDARDS AND IMPLICATIONS FOR INSTRUCTION

In this section, the text of each standard for mathematical practice is listed (CCSSI, 2010) along with a list of the practical implications of each standard for instruction and the classroom environment.

1. Make sense of problems and persevere in solving them

Mathematically proficient students start by explaining to themselves the meaning of a problem and looking for entry points to its solution. They analyze givens, constraints, relationships, and goals. They make conjectures about the form and meaning of the solution and plan a solution pathway rather than simply jumping into a solution attempt. They consider analogous problems, and try special cases and simpler forms of the original problem in order to gain insight into its solution. They monitor and evaluate their progress and change course if necessary. Older students might, depending on the context of the problem, transform algebraic expressions or change the viewing window on their graphing calculator to get the information they need. Mathematically proficient students can explain correspondences between equations, verbal descriptions, tables, and graphs or draw diagrams of important features and relationships, graph data, and search for regularity or trends. Younger students might rely on using concrete objects or pictures to help conceptualize and solve a problem. Mathematically proficient students check their answers to problems using a different method, and they continually ask themselves, "Does this make sense?" They can understand the approaches of others to solving complex problems and identify correspondences between different approaches.

Implications for instruction and the classroom environment:

- Students need to be engaged in problem solving on a regular basis.

- An instructional process is needed to build student capacity for problem solving.

- Problem solving should be about thinking and reasoning and should not be answer-driven.

- The problem-solving structure used needs to facilitate students sharing solutions, methods, and reasoning.

- The classroom environment should encourage student interaction and conversation that will lead to mathematical discourse.

- There should be an emphasis on student explanation to build strong metacognitive skills.

- Students need training in collaborative work.

- Create student success with problem solving early in the process. This will lead to a "productive disposition" toward mathematics—a belief that they can do it and that it makes sense.

- Expect verification or proof of solutions on a regular basis.

- There should be a structured approach to classroom problem solving to support student development in applying the math they are learning.

- Teachers need to allow students the opportunity to struggle with mathematical tasks rather than telling them how to find the solution as soon as there is any sign of frustration from the student.

- Instruction should emphasize equivalent representations of a given situation or mathematical relationship.

2. Reason abstractly and quantitatively

Mathematically proficient students make sense of quantities and their relationships in problem situations. They bring two complementary abilities to bear on problems involving quantitative relationships: the ability to decontextualize—to abstract a given situation and represent it symbolically and manipulate the representing symbols as if they have a life of their own, without necessarily attending to their referents—and the ability to contextualize, to pause as needed during the manipulation process in order to probe into the referents for the symbols involved. Quantitative reasoning entails habits of creating a coherent representation of the problem at hand; considering the units involved; attending to the meaning of quantities, not just how to compute them; and knowing and flexibly using different properties of operations and objects.

Implications for instruction and the classroom environment:

- Instruction has to be meaning-based. Students must feel that the math makes sense.

- The instructional program should facilitate development of number sense across all grades. Students need a strong sense of quantity and an understanding of the basis of the number system and the patterns in that system.

- This standard assumes students are involved in problem-solving experiences on a regular basis.

- Instructionally, concepts are taught within context. Symbols always have meaning.

- Students should have opportunities to develop a representation of a mathematical problem on a regular basis.
- Procedural teaching is tied to an actual context.
- Manipulations of symbols, manipulations within equations, and so on, should always be attached to a context and meaning.
- In most classrooms, there should be much more practice with application of the concepts being learned.
- Lessons and activities in classroom instruction should emphasize reasoning as opposed to only learning procedures.

3. Construct viable arguments and critique the reasoning of others

Mathematically proficient students understand and use stated assumptions, definitions, and previously established results in constructing arguments. They make conjectures and build a logical progression of statements to explore the truth of their conjectures. They are able to analyze situations by breaking them into cases and can recognize and use counterexamples. They justify their conclusions, communicate them to others, and respond to the arguments of others. They reason inductively about data, making plausible arguments that take into account the context from which the data arose. Mathematically proficient students are also able to compare the effectiveness of two plausible arguments, distinguish correct logic or reasoning from that which is flawed, and—if there is a flaw in an argument—explain what it is.

Elementary students can construct arguments using concrete referents such as objects, drawings, diagrams, and actions. Such arguments can make sense and be correct, even though they are not generalized or made formal until later grades. Later, students learn to determine domains to which an argument applies. Students at all grades can listen to or read the arguments of others, decide whether they make sense, and ask useful questions to clarify or improve the arguments.

Implications for instruction and the classroom environment:

- This standard assumes that the classroom environment is one of regular student interaction and conversation, and that students are highly engaged with the mathematics that they are learning.

- The traditional "telling method" of instruction will not allow students to develop the skills listed in this standard.

- Students need practice with the language of argument, conjecture, and discourse. This is best done instructionally in problem-solving situations or by involving students in engaging mathematical tasks.

- Teachers and students need to value individual student statements, ideas, and opinions concerning mathematical ideas. The classroom environment will need to be risk-free in terms of students presenting a conjecture, proposing a strategy, defending a solution, and so on.

- Students need experience with creating and developing mathematical arguments. Instructionally, this is easiest to do in a structured problem-solving program.

- Daily lessons and activities should be structured to facilitate and encourage student discourse on a regular basis so that students think that math instruction involves thinking and discussing and sharing ideas. Easy strategies to use are to have students paraphrase information within a lesson, explain how they arrived at their solution to another student, and verify their solution (how do they know they are correct mathematically) with another student.

- Units of instruction should include problem-based activities to provide opportunities for students to develop the skills listed in this standard.

- Students should present their solutions and ideas on a regular basis.

- Instruction moves students beyond computation with data to the interpretation and analysis of the various displays and measures used with data.

- The classroom environment should support students in developing the capacity to share their arguments and to listen to others' arguments and respond appropriately to those arguments.

4. Model with mathematics

Mathematically proficient students can apply the mathematics they know to solve problems arising in everyday life, society, and the workplace. In early grades, this might be as simple as writing an addition equation to describe a situation. In middle grades, a student might apply proportional reasoning to plan a school event or analyze a problem in the community. By high school, a student might use geometry to solve a design problem or use a function to describe how one quantity of interest depends on another. Mathematically proficient students who can apply what they know are comfortable making assumptions and approximations to simplify a complicated situation, realizing that these may need revision later. They are able to identify important quantities in a practical situation and map their relationships using such tools as diagrams, two-way tables, graphs, flowcharts and formulas. They can analyze those relationships mathematically to draw conclusions. They routinely interpret their mathematical results in the context of the situation and reflect on whether the results make sense, possibly improving the model if it has not served its purpose.

Implications for instruction and the classroom environment
(Adapted from NCTM, 2000):

Primary grades:

- Have students use physical objects, drawings, and physical gestures to represent situations.

- Have students represent ideas with objects that can be moved and rearranged. Encourage student verbal descriptions.

- Allow students to see different ways to represent the same situation.

- Help students see similarities in ways to represent different situations.

- Involve students in activities in which they create evidence of what they did to solve a problem. Have students share their representations.

- Teachers should be careful to not assume that students understand a diagram or equation the same way that they understand the representation. Young students interpret representations much differently than adults.

Upper elementary grades:

- Expect students to begin creating representations that are more detailed and accurate.

- Provide lots of practice with equations to help with understanding the equal sign.

- Model multiple representations for a given mathematical situation.

- Provide practice opportunities with a given representation in many contexts.

Middle school:

- Help students create representations that blend visual and numerical information.

- Use several representational forms for fractions, decimals, and percents.

- Provide lessons and activities that allow students to become familiar with a range of representations for linear relationships.

- Have students practice representing a given contextual situation in multiple ways.

- Use technology to examine relationships among different representations of a given linear function.

- Provide opportunities for students to solve applied problems to use the math that they know and to demonstrate the utility of various representations of information. Students could solve problems related to community, school, or classroom issues.

High school:

- Provide learning opportunities that allow students to see that different representations support different ways of thinking about and manipulating mathematical objects.

- Provide practice with converting among representations for a given situation to create flexibility with modeling.

- Emphasize selection of a certain representation for a mathematical situation based on what information the representation needs to convey.

5. Use appropriate tools strategically

Mathematically proficient students consider the available tools when solving a mathematical problem. These tools might include pencil and paper, concrete models, a ruler, a protractor, a calculator, a spreadsheet, a computer algebra system, a statistical package, or dynamic geometry software. Proficient students are sufficiently familiar with tools appropriate for their grade or course to make sound decisions about when each of these tools might be helpful, recognizing both the insight to be gained and their limitations. For example, mathematically proficient high school students analyze graphs of functions and solutions generated using a graphing calculator. They detect possible errors by strategically using estimation and other mathematical knowledge. When making mathematical models, they know that technology can enable them to visualize the results of varying assumptions, explore consequences, and compare predictions with data. Mathematically proficient students at various grade levels are able to identify relevant external mathematical resources, such as digital content located on a Web site, and use them to pose or solve problems. They are able to use technological tools to explore and deepen their understanding of concepts.

Implications for instruction and the classroom environment:

- Provide mathematical tools in the classroom.
- Make sure that students know how to use the available tools effectively.
- Discuss the impact of the use of tools on the solution.
- Discuss criteria to use to make a decision about when to use a mathematical tool.
- Provide problem-solving opportunities when students have the option to use tools to find a solution. Provide activities for which collaborative groups would make the decision to use tools or not.
- Have students include their rationale for using a tool in their explanation of their solution.

6. Attend to precision

Mathematically proficient students try to communicate precisely to others. They try to use clear definitions in discussion with others and in their own reasoning. They state the meaning of the symbols they choose, including using the equal sign consistently and appropriately. They are careful about specifying units of measure, and labeling axes to clarify the correspondence with quantities in a problem. They calculate accurately and efficiently, and express numerical answers with a degree of precision appropriate for the problem context. In the elementary grades, students give carefully formulated explanations to each other. By the time they reach high school, they have learned to examine claims and make explicit use of definitions.

Implications for instruction and the classroom environment:

- Mathematical vocabulary for the unit of instruction should be specifically taught and expected in classroom instruction and discussion.

- The classroom environment should encourage and expect mathematical discourse and student presentation of their ideas and solutions.

- Instruction about the meaning of mathematical symbols should be embedded in all lessons and activities.

- Number sense development should be reinforced on a regular basis from the standpoint of evaluating the reasonableness of the answer.

• Answers should be discussed in terms of the context of the problem to give students experience with the idea of level of precision.

• A systematic review process for computational skills that includes error analysis and feedback should be part of daily math instruction to develop student accuracy and proficiency.

7. Look for and make use of structure

Mathematically proficient students look closely to discern a pattern or structure. Young students, for example, might notice that three and seven more is the same amount as seven and three more, or they may sort a collection of shapes according to how many sides the shapes have. Later, students see 7×8 equals the well remembered $7 \times 5 + 7 \times 3$, in preparation for learning about the distributive property. In the expression $x^2 + 9x + 14$, older students can see the 14 as 2×7 and the 9 as $2 + 7$. They recognize the significance of an existing line in a geometric figure and can use the strategy of drawing an auxiliary line for solving problems. They also can step back for an overview and shift perspective. They can see complicated things, such as some algebraic expressions, as single objects or as being composed of several objects. For example, they can see $5 - 3(x - y)^2$ as 5 minus a positive number times a square and use that to realize that its value cannot be more than 5 for any real numbers x and y.

Implications for instruction and the classroom environment:

• Create a classroom environment where students always look for a pattern or an opportunity for generalization.

- Use lessons and activities that use pattern or structure to help develop conceptual understanding.

- Use mental math activities to practice patterns in the number system that can be useful to students.

- Use mathematical tasks that generate data that can be used to develop a generalization.

- This standard depends on a classroom environment that values and encourages student reasoning and sharing of student ideas as opposed to a teacher "telling" students how to do a skill or what the student should notice.

8. Look for and express regularity in repeated reasoning

Mathematically proficient students notice if calculations are repeated and look for both general methods and shortcuts. Upper elementary students might notice when dividing 25 by 11 that they are repeating the same calculations over and over again, and conclude they have a repeating decimal. By paying attention to the calculation of slope as they repeatedly check whether points are on the line through $(1, 2)$ with slope 3, middle school students might abstract the equation $(y - 2)/(x - 1) = 3$. Noticing the regularity in the way terms cancel when expanding $(x - 1)(x + 1)$, $(x - 1)(x^2 + x + 1)$, and $(x - 1)(x^3 + x^2 + x + 1)$ might lead them to the general formula for the sum of a geometric series. As they work to solve a problem, mathematically proficient students maintain oversight of the process, while attending to the details. They continually evaluate the reasonableness of their intermediate results.

Implications for instruction and the classroom environment:

Note: This standard uses the term "repeated reasoning" to mean that a calculation or process is repeated while solving a mathematical situation and that that repetition can be used to reach a generalization.

- Create a classroom environment where students always look for a pattern or an opportunity for generalization within computational skills.

- Use lessons and activities that use pattern or structure to help develop conceptual understanding.

- Use mental math activities to practice patterns in the number system that can be useful to students in developing more efficient methods for computation.

- Use mathematical tasks that generate data that can be used to develop a generalization specific to a computational procedure.

- This standard depends on a classroom environment that values and encourages student reasoning and sharing of student ideas as opposed to a teacher "telling" students how to do a skill or what the student should notice.

MATHEMATICAL PRACTICE STANDARDS WITH EXAMPLES OF MATCHING CONTENT STANDARDS

In the introduction to the Common Core State Standards for Mathematics, the authors provide information about the connection between the practice standards and the content standards.

> In this respect, those content standards which set an expectation of understanding are potential "points of

intersection" between the Standards for Mathematical Content and the Standards for Mathematical Practice. (CCSSI, 2010, p. 8)

To illustrate how the content standards are influenced by the philosophy used to develop the practice standards, several content standards from various grade levels are listed that match each of the mathematical practice standards. The portion of the content standard that emphasizes the practice standard expectation is *italicized*.

1. Make sense of problems and persevere in solving them

1.OA.1—Use addition and subtraction within 20 *to solve word problems* involving situations of adding to, taking away from, putting together, taking apart, and comparing, with unknowns in all positions, e.g., by using objects, drawings, and equations with a symbol for the unknown number to represent the problem.

3.MD.8—*Solve real-world and mathematical problems* involving perimeters of polygons, including finding the perimeter given the side lengths, finding unknown side length, and exhibiting rectangles with the same perimeters and different areas or the same area and different perimeters.

3.OA.8—*Solve two-step word problems using the four operations.* Represent these problems using equations with a letter standing for the unknown quantity. Assess the reasonableness of answers using mental computation and estimation strategies including rounding.

5.NF.6—*Solve real-world problems involving multiplication of fractions* and mixed numbers, e.g., by using visual fraction models or equations to represent the problem.

2. Reason abstractly and quantitatively

K.CC.4—Understand the *relationship between numbers and quantities*: connect counting to cardinality.

4.OA.3—Solve multistep word problems posed with whole numbers and having whole-number answers using the four operations, including problems in which remainders must be interpreted. *Represent these problems using equations with a letter standing for the unknown quantity.* Assess the reasonableness of answers using mental computation and estimation strategies including rounding.

5.NF.6—Solve real-world problems involving multiplication of fractions and mixed numbers, e.g., *by using visual fraction models or equations to represent the problem.*

6.EE.6—*Use variables to represent numbers and write expressions when solving a real-world or mathematical problem;* understand that a variable can represent an unknown number, or, depending on the purpose at hand, any number in a specified set.

6.EE.2—*Write, read, and evaluate expressions in which letters stand for numbers.*

3. Construct viable arguments and critique the reasoning of others

4.NF.1—*Explain why a fraction a/b is equivalent to a fraction (n × a)/(n × b) by using visual fraction models, with attention to how the number and size of the parts differ even though the two fractions themselves are the same size.* Use this principle to recognize and generate equivalent fractions.

7.SP.3—*Informally assess the degree of visual overlap of two numerical data distributions with similar variabilities, measuring the difference between the centers by expressing it as a multiple of a measure of variability.* For example, the mean height of players on the basketball team is 10 cm greater than the mean height of players on the soccer team, about twice the variability (mean absolute deviation) on either team; on a dot plot, the separation between the two distributions of heights is noticeable.

7.SP.4—*Use measures of center and measures of variability for numerical data from random samples to draw informal comparative inferences about two populations.* For example, decide whether the words in a chapter of a seventh-grade science book are generally longer than the words in a chapter of a fourth-grade science book.

4. Model with mathematics

3.MD.3—*Draw a scaled picture graph and a scaled bar graph to represent a data set with several categories.* Solve one- and two-step "how many more" and "how many less" problems using information presented in scaled bar graphs. *For example, draw a bar graph in which each square in the bar graph might represent 5 pets.*

4.NF.4c—Solve word problems involving multiplication of a fraction by a whole number, e.g., *by using visual fraction models and equations to represent the problem.* For example, if each person at a party will eat 3/8 of a pound of roast beef, and there will be 5 people at the party, how many pounds of roast beef will be needed? Between what two whole numbers does your answer lie?

6.EE.9—Use variables to represent two quantities in a real-world problem that change in relationship to one another; write an equation to express one quantity, thought of as the dependent variable, in terms of the other quantity, thought of as the independent variable. *Analyze the relationship between the dependent and independent variables using graphs and tables, and relate these to the equation.* For example, in a problem involving motion at constant speed, list and graph ordered pairs of distances and times, and write the equation $d = 65t$ to represent the relationship between distance and time.

5. Use appropriate tools strategically

K.OA.1—Represent addition and subtraction with *objects, fingers, mental images, drawings, sounds, acting out situations, verbal explanations, expressions, or equations.*

7.G.2—Draw (freehand, with *ruler and protractor, and with technology*) geometric shapes with given conditions. Focus on constructing triangles from three measures of angles or sides, noticing when the conditions determine a unique triangle, more than one triangle, or no triangle.

5.NBT.7—Add, subtract, multiply, and divide decimals to hundredths, using *concrete models or drawings* and strategies based on place value, properties of operations, and/or the relationship between addition and subtraction; relate the strategy to a written method and explain the reasoning used.

6. Attend to precision

K.OA.5—*Fluently* add and subtract within 5.

1.OA.7—Understand the *meaning of the equal sign* and determine if equations involving addition and subtraction are true or false.

3.OA.7—*Fluently* multiply and divide within 100, using strategies such as the relationship between multiplication and division (e.g., knowing that $8 \times 5 = 40$, one knows $40 \div 5 = 8$) or properties of operations. By the end of grade 3, know from memory all products of two one-digit numbers.

4.NBT.4—*Fluently* add and subtract multi-digit whole numbers using the standard algorithm.

5.NBT.5—*Fluently* multiply multi-digit whole numbers using the standard algorithm.

6.NS.3—*Fluently* add, subtract, multiply, and divide multi-digit decimals using the standard algorithm for each operation.

7. Look for and make use of structure

K.MD.1—Describe measurable attributes of objects, such as length or weight. *Describe several measurable attributes of a single object.*

1.OA.3—*Apply properties of operations* as strategies to add or subtract.

3.MD.7—*Relate area to the operations of multiplication and addition.*

5.MD.5—*Relate volume to the operations of multiplication and addition* and solve real-world and mathematical problems involving volume.

6.EE.3—*Apply the properties of operations* to generate equivalent expressions. For example, apply the distributive property to the expression $3(2 + x)$ to produce the equivalent expression $6 + 3x$; apply the distributive property to the expression $24x + 18y$ to produce the equivalent expression $6(4x + 3y)$; apply properties of operations to $y + y + y$ to produce the equivalent expression $3y$.

8. Look for and express regularity in repeated reasoning

4.NF.4—*Apply and extend previous understandings* of multiplication to multiply a fraction by a whole number.

5.NF.4b—Find the area of a rectangle with fractional side lengths by tiling it with unit squares of the appropriate unit fraction side lengths, and *show that the area is the same as would be found by multiplying the side lengths.* Multiply fractional side lengths to find areas of rectangles, and represent fraction products as rectangular areas.

7.NS.1—*Apply and extend previous understandings of addition and subtraction* to add and subtract rational numbers; represent addition and subtraction on a horizontal or vertical number line diagram.

GENERAL THEMES
FROM PRACTICE STANDARDS

From the previous examination of the standards for mathematical practice it becomes apparent that there are some instructional themes that are emphasized across the practice standards and the content standards. Development of these elements in instructional practice in mathematics classrooms will be a major factor in the successful implementation of the Common Core. The instructional themes that are emphasized are problem solving, reasoning and thinking, student engagement with mathematical ideas, applying previous understandings to a new concept, and mathematics being learned with understanding and within context.

These themes demonstrate that the Common Core standards were developed using the idea that students should understand the math that they are learning and that they should be able to use and apply the concepts that they understand. Instructionally, the Common Core promotes students being engaged with mathematics rather than being told how to do procedures. Students are expected to be able to connect what they have previously learned to a new concept, and to think and reason using the concepts and ideas that they do understand. Throughout the content standards, there is a major emphasis on student thinking and reasoning. The content standards contain terms such as "reason," "understand," "analyze," "solve," "apply and extend previous understanding," "interpret," and "explain," making it very clear what the authors of the Common Core standards feel is the key to student success in mathematics.

IMPACT ON THE CLASSROOM TEACHER

The standards for mathematical practice that accompany the standards for mathematical content in the Common Core present several challenges to classroom teachers of mathematics across the country. The practice standards assume that teachers have not only strong content knowledge in mathematics, but also strong knowledge about how students learn mathematics conceptually and procedurally. Most classroom teachers learned math procedurally, without necessarily understanding the concepts attached to the procedures. The practice standards also promote application of concepts being learned through problem solving, which again assumes that the classroom teacher is comfortable with mathematical problem solving and feels confident using problem solving instructionally.

Another challenge for many teachers will be the suggested shift in the classroom environment from a teacher-centered approach focused on teacher explanations to a student-engaging environment that utilizes student discourse, explanation, verification, collaboration, and metacognition to develop understanding of mathematical concepts. If a teacher has not experienced this type of classroom environment, it is not an easy transition. The bottom line is that teachers will have to examine how they think students effectively learn mathematics, what information that belief is based upon, and what training and support they need to make the necessary changes in their instructional practices.

HOW TO START IMPLEMENTING MATHEMATICAL PRACTICE STANDARDS

Following are a few suggestions on how to start integrating the standards of mathematical practice into classroom instruction.

- Promote student conversation about mathematics in your classroom on a daily basis.

- Start attending to student mistakes and misconceptions. Make it okay to make a mistake in your classroom.

- Expect that all students will learn mathematics. Let students know that you believe they will all learn math successfully. Expectations are very powerful.

- Create a balance of teacher talk and student talk. Listen more to student explanations.

- Start a structured problem-solving program that promotes regular problem solving.

- Promote student explanation of solutions in written and verbal forms.

- Start asking students to show or explain why their solution is correct mathematically.
- Use activities that utilize collaborative work.
- Use lessons and activities that involve students in the use of patterns and generalization from those patterns.

SUMMARY

The Common Core State Standards for Mathematics will present challenges to the classroom teacher that will run the gamut from interpreting the content standards to implementing the practice standards. The fortunate element of the challenge is that the practice standards and the content standards are directly linked and are based upon a common understanding of how students learn mathematics.

To successfully implement the Common Core content standards, it will be necessary for teachers to fully implement the practice standards, which are calling for a much-needed change in how math lessons are designed and delivered in U.S. classrooms. The practices match what research tells us about how students learn mathematics and how to promote an engaging classroom environment that will lead to student understanding of mathematical concepts. Students need to be involved in discussing math, applying math, verifying their solutions, and sharing their mathematical ideas, not just listening to a teacher's explanation, to successfully understand mathematics. The challenge of the Common Core is to not only interpret and implement the content standards, but to change the instructional environment in which the students learn the content standards. The mathematical practice standards provide the guidelines for that important instructional change to take place.

Integrating the Common Core practice standards with the content standards has tremendous potential to create effective classroom instruction and begin the process of helping all students be successful with mathematics.

References

Common Core State Standards Initiative (CCSSI). (2010, June). *Common Core State Standards for mathematics* (PDF document). Retrieved from www.corestandards.org/assets/CCSSI_Math %20Standards.pdf

National Council of Teachers of Mathematics (NCTM). (2000). *Principles and standards for school mathematics.* Reston, VA: NCTM.

National Council of Teachers of Mathematics (NCTM). (2009). *Focus in high school mathematics: Reasoning and sense making.* Reston, VA: NCTM.

National Council of Teachers of Mathematics (NCTM). (2010). *Making it happen: A guide to interpreting and implementing Common Core State Standards for mathematics.* Reston, VA: NCTM.

National Research Council. (2001). *Adding it up: Helping children learn mathematics.* J. Kilpatrick, J. Swafford, & B. Findell (Eds.). Mathematics Learning Study Committee, Center for Education, Division of Behavioral and Social Sciences Education. Washington, DC: National Academies Press.

Van de Walle, J. (2007). *Elementary and middle school mathematics— Teaching developmentally* (6th ed.). Boston, MA: Pearson.

Strategies for Addressing Rigor in the Mathematics Common Core

Cathy J. Lassiter

The Common Core State Standards for Mathematics require an increase in the rigor and scope, and a change in the focus, of mathematics instruction in American classrooms. In an analysis of the standards in July 2010, the Thomas B. Fordham Institute published a report detailing the content, rigor, articulation of concepts, and general organization of the work. The report stated that the development of arithmetic in elementary school is a primary focus of the standards. Fractions are developed rigorously, and place value is developed quite well (Carmichael, et al., 2010).

There are eight standards for mathematical practice that are consistent in grades K–12: 1. Make sense of problems and persevere in solving them; 2. Reason abstractly and quantitatively; 3. Construct viable arguments and critique the reasoning of others; 4. Model with mathematics; 5. Use appropriate tools strategically; 6. Attend to precision; 7. Look for and make use of structures; and 8. Look for and express regularity in repeated reasoning (CCSSI, 2010a). These eight standards of practice are combined with content standards that endeavor to balance procedure and understanding.

The Fordham analysis concluded that the math Common Core sets excellent priorities that are expressed both explicitly and implicitly (Carmichael, et al., 2010). In the elementary grades, explicit guidance is provided by identifying the three or four main areas that students are expected to master. The standards also make it crystal clear that arithmetic is the most important math topic in the early grades. The standards insist that students learn math facts that are foundational to their success in higher levels. Instant recall of the number facts is required for addition and multiplication, and students are expected to become "fluent" with numbers and operations. The standards discourage the use of calculators in the elementary grades (Carmichael, et al., 2010). Word problems, including multistep problems, are introduced early and included throughout. In middle school, work with fractions and decimals is well utilized in the coverage of proportions, percents, rates, and ratios, and the standards and approach are highly rigorous. High school geometry is also lauded for good coverage of content, and proofs are included throughout the standards. Although a few concerns are noted about organization of the high school content and the omission of explicit foundations for geometry, the rigor of the math Common Core is graded high (Carmichael, et al., 2010). In order for teachers to meet the challenges of the new standards they will have to adjust their teaching practices, and in some cases adopt new approaches, if they hope to be successful in meeting the year-end requirements for student mastery.

STRATEGIES FOR TEACHING THE MATH CCSS

The teaching strategies in this section are recommended by the National Council of Teachers of Mathematics (NCTM).

These strategies provide a solid foundation as teachers strive to strengthen their instructional delivery to achieve success in the mathematics Common Core.

Teaching Strategy 1: Create "Worthwhile" Problems as a Foundation for Daily Instruction

According to research compiled by the National Council of Teachers of Mathematics, problem solving should be taught as early as preschool, in every grade level, in every mathematics topic, and in every lesson. It should not be taught as an isolated topic. The Common Core authors agree with this axiom and have made problem solving the cornerstone of the math standards. John Hattie, researcher and author of *Visible Learning*, a meta-analysis of more than 800 meta-analyses on instruction, involving millions of students and 15 years of research, found high effect sizes (defined as .4 or higher) for improving student achievement when problem solving methods were used. He states, "A format consisting of full problem statements supported by diagrams, figures, or sketches directly related to higher performance" (Hattie, 2009, p. 210).

When teachers think of problem solving, they often think of story or word problems. But the NCTM cautions that not all word problems are "problematic" enough for students. In general, the term "problem solving" refers to mathematical tasks that have the potential to provide intellectual challenges that can enhance students' mathematical development. These problems can promote students' conceptual understanding, foster their ability to reason and communicate mathematically, and capture their interest and curiosity (Cai and Lester, 2011). The challenge for teachers is knowing how to effectively implement problem solving as a prominent part of their curriculum and daily lessons. Another challenge is creating "worthwhile" problems that stimulate higher-level thinking and significant mathematical development. Exhibit 4.1 lists criteria developed by the NCTM to assist teachers in choosing, revising, and designing problems that are "worthwhile."

The first four criteria are considered by the NCTM as critical in the selection of all problems. The other criteria will come into play depending on the instructional purpose of the problem-solving lesson. The requirements of the CCSS in both literacy and math direct that criteria 7 and 8 also be considered essential in creating worthwhile problems for students. If teachers are to incorporate worthwhile problems, however, they must dedicate the

BOOK THREE EXHIBIT 4.1 **Criteria for Creating Worthwhile Problems**

1. The problem has important, useful mathematics embedded in it.
2. The problem requires higher level thinking and problem solving.
3. The problem contributes to the conceptual development of students.
4. The problem creates an opportunity for the teacher to assess what his or her students are learning and where they are experiencing difficulty.
5. The problem can be approached by students in multiple ways using different strategy solutions.
6. The problem has various solutions or allows different decisions or positions to be taken and defended.
7. The problem encourages student engagement and discourse.
8. The problem connects to other mathematical ideas.
9. The problem promotes the skillful use of mathematics.
10. The problem provides an opportunity to practice important skills.

Source: Cai and Lester, 2011.

time needed to do an effective job with them. Students need time to think, ponder, discuss, and ask questions. They need time to effectively struggle with the problem to deepen their understanding. Teachers all too often give the answers to students during the struggle. When they tell students how to solve a problem, teachers remove the challenge and take over the thinking and reasoning. It is important for students to be encouraged to use any approach they can think of, draw on any knowledge they have, and justify their ideas when solving problems. This approach facilitates social interactions, meaningful negotiation, and shared understandings (Cai and Lester, 2011). Exhibits 4.2 and 4.3 provide examples of

BOOK
THREE
**EXHIBIT
4.2**

**Sample Mathematics Standards
Relating to Problem Solving**

Common Core Mathematics Standards	
Grade Level and Standard Number	**Standard Text**
Grade 2 2.OA.1	Use addition and subtraction within 100 to solve one- and two-step word problems involving situations of adding to, taking from, putting together, taking apart, and comparing with unknowns in all positions, e.g., by using drawings and equations with a symbol for the unknown number to represent the problem.
Grade 6 6.NS.1	Interpret and compute quotients of fractions, and solve word problems involving division of fractions by fractions, e.g., by using visual fraction models and equations to represent the problem.
High School Geometry G-MG.3	Apply geometric methods to solve design problems (e.g., designing an object or structure to satisfy physical constraints or minimize cost; working with typographic grid systems based on ratios).

Source: CCSSI, 2010a.

Sample Literacy Standards Relating to Instructional Methods to Teach Problem Solving

Common Core Literacy Standards (Speaking and Listening)	
Grade Level and Standard Number	**Standard Text**
Kindergarten SL.K.1a	Follow agreed-upon rules for discussion (e.g., listening to others and taking turns speaking about the topics and texts under discussion).
Grade 3 SL.3.1c,d	Ask questions to check for understanding of information presented, stay on topic, and link comments to the remarks of others. Explain their own ideas and understanding in light of the discussion.
Grade 8 SL.8.1d	Acknowledge new information expressed by others, and when warranted, qualify or justify their own views in light of the evidence presented.
Grades 11–12 SL.11–12.1	Initiate and participate effectively in a range of collaborative discussions (one-on-one, in groups, and teacher-led) with diverse partners on grade 11–12 topics, texts, and issues, building on others' ideas and expressing their own ideas clearly and persuasively.

Source: CCSSI, 2010b.

standards from the Common Core related to the instructional strategies for problem solving.

Teaching Strategy 2: Use Real Data and Current Events to Make Mathematics More Engaging and Relevant

The oil spill in the Gulf of Mexico in April 2010 is an excellent example of a current event applicable to mathematics instruction.

Creative math teachers could use maps and surface area to engage students in creating their own problems and solutions. Students must defend their solutions and apply them to the real event. Teachers could use the oil spill to discuss topics such as percents, proportionality, linear relationships, domain, discrete vs. continuous data sets, and piecewise functions.

The National Council of Teachers of Mathematics asserts that students who study news and current events in school do better on standardized tests and develop and improve reading, vocabulary, math, and social studies skills. The council recommends that math teachers use the newspaper as a source for data sets to teach box and whisker plots or linear regression. Teachers should use multiple representations of the same data to show how different representations give different information. Students should see a mixture of tables, graphs, words, symbols, and pictures. They should be asked to create several depictions for themselves and weigh out the advantages and disadvantages of each and make an argument of which works best in certain circumstances. Other recommended strategies include designing lessons that engage students in prediction using data. For example, look at population growth in your city or state and have students predict, based on the trend data, what the population will be in 10 years, 50 years, or 100 years (NCTM, 2011a).

Exhibits 4.4 and 4.5 provide a sample list of Common Core standards that are related to using real data and current events in mathematics instruction.

**Sample Mathematics Standards
Addressed by Using Real Data**

Common Core Mathematics Standards	
Grade Level and Standard Number	**Standard Text**
Kindergarten K.G.1	Describe objects in the environment using names of shapes, and describe the relative positions of these objects using terms such as *above, below, beside, in front of, behind,* and *next to.*
Grade 4 4.MD.2	Use four operations to solve word problems involving distances, intervals of time, liquid volumes, masses of objects, and money, including problems involving simple fractions or decimals, and problems that require expressing measurements given in a larger unit in terms of a smaller unit. Represent measurement quantities using diagrams such as a number line diagrams that feature a measurement scale.
Grade 7 7.NS.3	Solve real-world and mathematical problems involving the four operations with rational numbers.
High School Statistics and Probability S-ID.4	Use mean and standard deviation of a data set to fit it to a normal distribution and to estimate population percentages. Recognize that there are data sets for which such a procedure is not appropriate. Use calculators, spreadsheets, and tables to estimate areas under the normal curve.

Source: CCSSI, 2010a.

Sample Literacy Standards Addressed by Using Real Data

Common Core Literacy Standards (Science and Technical Subjects)	
Grade Level and Standard Number	**Standard Text**
Grades 6–8 RST.6–8.3	Follow precisely a multistep procedure when carrying out experiments, taking measurements, or performing technical tasks.
Grades 9–10 RST.9–10.3	Follow precisely a complex multistep procedure when carrying out experiments, taking measurements, or performing technical tasks, attending to special cases or exceptions defined in the text.
Grades 11–12 RST.11–12.3	Follow precisely a complex multistep procedure when carrying out experiments, taking measurements, or performing technical tasks; analyze specific results based on explanations in the text.

Source: CCSSI, 2010b.

Teaching Strategy 3: Ask Quality Questions and Promote Discourse

The following questioning techniques are recommended by the NCTM to promote higher-order thinking and promote appropriate discourse in the math classroom (NCTM, 2011b):

Pose an unanswered question to challenge students. Provide time for them to ponder, research, and discuss the question. Encourage them to offer speculations and assumptions. Afterward, tell students the question has no solution or right answer. This activity prepares them for mathematics in life.

Not every question or problem has one right answer that is neat and clean.

Leave a question unanswered at the end of class. This will give students time to ponder and consider many answers before the next class period. Doing this may be uncomfortable for the teacher at first, but oftentimes teachers provide answers far too quickly, which denies students the benefit of the challenge and exercise for their brains.

Give students the answer to a problem or question and ask them to come up with the question. An example for younger students may be to write a story in which the answer is 20 cookies and that requires subtraction. For older students, the mathematics would be more complex and the story more detailed. Students could trade papers and attempt to solve each others' problems. A follow-up discussion might include what information was irrelevant, what parts were difficult to follow, or what elements provided clues to the answer.

When using games in class, ask follow-up questions. Questions should include asking students to share what strategy they used during the game and why. Ask them to explain their reasoning and their strategy.

Teach students to acknowledge and pursue the struggle and process of learning. Students are done a disservice when they are presented with questions they already know how to solve. They need to struggle with questions they do not know how to solve to develop deeper mathematical understandings. Support and encouragement through the struggle will keep them engaged in the challenge.

Exhibits 4.6 and 4.7 provide examples of Common Core standards that are addressed when the teacher uses quality questions to promote discourse.

BOOK THREE EXHIBIT 4.6

Sample Mathematics Standards Addressed by Using Quality Questions/Discourse

Common Core Mathematics Standards	
Grade Level and Standard Number	**Standard Text**
Grade 1 1.NBT.6	Subtract multiples of 10 in the range 10–90 from multiples of 10 in the range of 10–90 (positive or zero differences) using concrete models or drawings and strategies based on place value, properties of operations, and/or the relationship between addition and subtraction; relate the strategy to a written method and explain the reasoning used.
Grade 3 3.OA.8	Solve two-step word problems using the four operations. Represent these problems using equations with a letter standing for the unknown quantity. Assess the reasonableness of answers using mental computation and estimation strategies including rounding.
Grade 8 8.G.7	Apply the Pythagorean Theorem to determine unknown side lengths in right triangles in real-world and mathematical problems in two and three dimensions.
High School Number and Quantity N-RN.1	Explain how the definition of the meaning of rational exponents follows from extending the properties of integer exponents to those values, allowing for a notation for radicals in terms of rational exponents.

Source: CCSSI, 2010a.

Sample Literacy Standards
Addressed by Using Quality Questions/Discourse

Common Core Literacy Standards (Reading Informational Text)	
Grade Level and Standard Number	**Standard Text**
Grade 2 RI.2.4	Determine the meaning of words and phrases in a text relevant to a grade 2 topic or subject.
Grade 5 RI.5.5	Compare and contrast the overall structure (e.g., chronology, comparison, cause/effect, problem/solution) of events, ideas, concepts or information in two or more texts.
Grade 7 RI.7.9	Analyze how two or more authors writing about the same topic shape their presentations of key information by emphasizing different evidence or advancing different interpretations of facts.
Grades 9–10 RI.9–10.8	Delineate and evaluate the argument and specific claims in a text, assessing whether the reasoning is valid and the evidence is relevant and sufficient; identify false statements and fallacious reasoning.

Source: CCSSI, 2010b.

SUMMARY

The Common Core State Standards are designed to ensure that all American students graduate from high school ready for college and careers. They are internationally benchmarked and raise the bar on what is expected of our students and when it is expected. Both the English language arts and math standards require that our students solve complex problems, think critically, read and write proficiently, and develop and defend their ideas effectively.

The Common Core mathematics standards focus on the development of arithmetic in elementary school. Fractions are developed rigorously, and arithmetic is the most important math topic in the early grades. Guidance is provided by identifying the three or four main areas that students are expected to master in the elementary grades. The standards insist that students learn math facts, and fluency with number facts is required for addition and multiplication. Word problems are introduced early and are a focus throughout the standards. In middle school, work with fractions and decimals are covered in proportions, percents, rates, and ratios. Teaching practices will have to change to prepare students for the rigors of the new standards.

The National Council of Teachers of Mathematics has published suggested teaching strategies that align with the Common Core mathematics standards.

Teaching Strategy 1: Create "worthwhile" problems as a foundation for daily instruction.

Teaching Strategy 2: Use real data and current events to make mathematics more engaging and relevant.

Teaching Strategy 3: Ask quality questions and promote discourse.

Incorporating teaching strategies that focus on problem solving, keep students engaged, and promote discourse results in lessons that are rigorous enough to help students achieve the high expectations laid out in the Common Core State Standards for Mathematics.

References

Cai, J., & Lester, F. (2011). *Why is teaching with problem solving important to student learning?* National Council of Teachers of Mathematics (NCTM) brief. Retrieved from www.nctm.org/news/content.aspx?id=25713

Carmichael, S., Martino, G., Porter-Magee, K., & Wilson, W. (2010). *The state of state standards—and the Common Core—in 2010.* Washington, DC: Thomas B. Fordham Institute.

Common Core State Standards Initiative (CCSSI). (2010a, June). *Common Core State Standards for mathematics* (PDF document). Retrieved from www.corestandards.org/assets/CCSSI_Math%20Standards.pdf

Common Core State Standards Initiative (CCSSI). (2010b, June). *Common Core State Standards for English language arts & literacy in history/social studies, science, and technical subjects* (PDF document). Retrieved from www.corestandards.org/assets/CCSSI_ELA%20Standards.pdf

Hattie, J. (2009). *Visible learning: A synthesis of over 800 meta-analyses relating to achievement.* New York: Routledge.

National Council of Teachers of Mathematics (NCTM). (2011a). *Tips on using real data and current events.* Retrieved from www.nctm.org/resources/content.aspx?id=16263

National Council of Teachers of Mathematics (NCTM). (2011b). *Asking questions and promoting discourse.* Retrieved from www.nctm.org/resources/content.aspx?id=25149 and www.nctm.org/resources/content.aspx?id=25150

Appendices Overview

APPENDIX A: *Critical Areas of Focus*

Appendix A features an overview of the critical areas of focus for K–8 mathematics instructional time. The Common Core State Standards for Mathematics have been designed around the principles of focus, clarity, and specificity. In response to this challenge, the K–8 grade-specific standards begin with an introduction for each grade level articulating two to four critical areas of focus per grade level.

APPENDIX B: *Grade-Specific Expectations*

Appendix B displays several K–8 grade-specific standards from the perspective of examining ways in which students are expected to "show what they know." The examples in Appendix B feature grade-specific standards that integrate verbal explanations and descriptions, as well as grade-specific standards that require students to apply mathematics to solve real-world and mathematical problems. Included are:

- K–8 Verbal Explanations, Verbal Descriptions, Explaining, Justifying
- K–8 Solving Word Problems
- K–8 Solving Real-World and Mathematical Problems

APPENDIX C: *Points of Intersection*

Appendix C features both the K–8 grade-specific standards and the high school conceptual categories that begin with the word "understand." Why? According to the Common Core State Standards for Mathematics document, "the Standards for Mathematical Content are a balanced combination of procedure and understanding. Expectations that begin with the word 'understand' are often especially good opportunities to connect the practices to the content."

"In this respect, those content standards which set an expectation of understanding are potential 'points of intersection' between the Standards for Mathematical Content and the Standards for Mathematical Practice" (CCSSI, 2010, p. 8).

APPENDIX D: *High School Modeling Standards*

Appendix D features the high school modeling standards that are embedded in the other conceptual category content standards.

"Modeling is best interpreted not as a collection of isolated topics but in relation to other standards. Making mathematical models is a Standard for Mathematical Practice, and specific modeling standards appear throughout the high school standards indicated by a star symbol (*). The star symbol sometimes appears on the heading for a group of standards; in that case, it should be understood to apply to all standards in that group" (CCSSI, 2010, p. 57).

APPENDIX E: *High School Advanced Mathematics Standards*

Appendix E features the high school mathematics standards students should learn in order to take advanced mathematics courses.

"The high school standards specify the mathematics that all students should study in order to be college and career ready. Additional mathematics that students should learn in order to take advanced courses such as calculus, advanced statistics, or discrete mathematics is indicated by (+), as in this example:

> (+) Represent complex numbers on the complex plane in rectangular and polar form (including real and imaginary numbers).

All standards without a (+) symbol should be in the common mathematics curriculum for all college and career ready students. Standards with a (+) symbol may also appear in courses intended for all students" (CCSSI, 2010, p. 57).

References

Common Core State Standards Initiative (CCSSI). (2010, June). *Common Core State Standards for mathematics* (PDF document). Retrieved from www.corestandards.org/assets/CCSSI_Math %20Standards.pdf

Critical Areas of Focus

	Instructional time should focus on these critical areas:
Kindergarten	1. Representing, relating, and operating on whole numbers, initially with sets of objects.
	2. Describing shapes and space.
More learning time in Kindergarten should be devoted to number than to other topics.	
Grade 1	1. Developing understanding of addition, subtraction, and strategies for addition and subtraction within 20.
	2. Developing understanding of whole number relationships and place value, including grouping in tens and ones.
	3. Developing understanding of linear measurement and measuring lengths as iterating length units.
	4. Reasoning about attributes of, and composing and decomposing geometric shapes.
Grade 2	1. Extending understanding of base-ten notation.
	2. Building fluency with addition and subtraction.
	3. Using standard units of measure.
	4. Describing and analyzing shapes.
Grade 3	1. Developing understanding of multiplication and division and strategies for multiplication and division within 100.
	2. Developing understanding of fractions, especially unit fractions (fractions with numerator 1).
	3. Developing understanding of the structure of rectangular arrays and of area.
	4. Describing and analyzing two-dimensional shapes.
Grade 4	1. Developing understanding and fluency with multi-digit multiplication and developing understanding of dividing to find quotients involving multi-digit dividends.
	2. Developing an understanding of fraction equivalence, addition and subtraction of fractions with like denominators, and multiplication of fractions by whole numbers.
	3. Understanding that geometric figures can be analyzed and classified based on their properties, such as having parallel sides, perpendicular sides, particular angle measures, and symmetry.

Grade 5	1. Developing fluency with addition and subtraction of fractions, and developing understanding of the multiplication of fractions and of division of fractions in limited cases (unit fractions divided by whole numbers and whole numbers divided by unit fractions).
	2. Extending division to 2-digit divisors, integrating decimal fractions into the place value system and developing understanding of operations with decimals to hundredths, and developing fluency with whole number and decimal operations.
	3. Developing understanding of volume.
Grade 6	1. Connecting ratio and rate to whole number multiplication and division and using concepts of ratio and rate to solve problems.
	2. Completing understanding of division of fractions and extending the notion of number to the system of rational numbers, which includes negative numbers.
	3. Writing, interpreting, and using expressions and equations.
	4. Developing understanding of statistical thinking.
Grade 7	1. Developing understanding of and applying proportional relationships.
	2. Developing understanding of operations with rational numbers and working with expressions and linear equations.
	3. Solving problems involving scale drawings and informal geometric constructions, and working with two- and three-dimensional shapes to solve problems involving area, surface area, and volume.
	4. Drawing inferences about population based on samples.
Grade 8	1. Formulating and reasoning about expressions and equations, including modeling an association in bivariate data with a linear equation, and solving linear equations and systems of linear equations.
	2. Grasping the concept of a function and using functions to describe quantitative relationships.
	3. Analyzing two- and three-dimensional space and figures using distance, angle, similarity, and congruence, and understanding and applying the Pythagorean Theorem.

Source: Common Core State Standards for Mathematics (CCSSI, 2010, pp. 9, 13, 17, 21, 27, 33, 41, 46, 52).

APPENDIX B

Grade-Specific Expectations

K–8 Verbal Explanations, Verbal Descriptions, Explaining, Justifying		
Counting and Cardinality		
Kindergarten	K.CC.1	**Count** to 100 by ones and by tens.
	K.CC.2	**Count** forward beginning from a given number within the known sequence (instead of having to begin at 1).
	K.CC.4a	a. When counting objects, **say** the number names in the standard order, pairing each object with one and only one number name and each number name with one and only one object.
	K.CC.5	**Count** to answer "how many?" questions about as many as 20 things arranged in a line, a rectangular array, or a circle, or as many as 10 things in a scattered configuration; given a number from 1–20, count out that many objects.
Operations and Algebraic Thinking		
Kindergarten	K.OA.1	Represent addition and subtraction with objects, fingers, mental images, drawings, sounds (e.g., claps), acting out situations, **verbal explanations**, expressions, or equations.
Grade 3	3.OA.9	Identify arithmetic patterns (including patterns in the addition table or multiplication table), and **explain** them using properties of operations. *For example, observe that 4 times a number is always even, and explain why 4 times a number can be decomposed into two equal addends.*
Number and Operations in Base Ten		
Grade 1	1.NBT.1	**Count** to 120, starting at any number less than 120. In this range, read and write numerals and represent a number of objects with a written numeral.
	1.NBT.4	Add within 100, including adding a two-digit number and a one-digit number, and adding a two-digit number and a multiple of 10, using concrete models or drawings and strategies based on place value, properties of operations, and/or the relationship between addition and subtraction; relate the strategy to a written method and **explain the reasoning used**. Understand that in adding two-digit numbers, one adds tens and tens, ones and ones; and sometimes it is necessary to compose a ten.
	1.NBT.5	Given a two-digit number, mentally find 10 more or 10 less than the number, without having to count; **explain the reasoning used.**
	1.NBT.6	Subtract multiples of 10 in the range 10–90 from multiples of 10 in the range 10–90 (positive or zero differences), using concrete models or drawings and strategies based on place value, properties of operations, and/or the relationship between addition and subtraction; relate the strategy to a written method and **explain the reasoning used.**

K–8 Verbal Explanations, Verbal Descriptions, Explaining, Justifying
(continued)

Number and Operations in Base Ten *(continued)*

Grade 2	**2.NBT.2**	**Count** within 1000; skip-count by 5s, 10s, and 100s.
	2.NBT.9	**Explain why** addition and subtraction strategies work, using place value and the properties of operations.
Grade 4	**4.NBT.5**	Multiply a whole number of up to four digits by a one-digit whole number, and multiply two two-digit numbers, using strategies based on place value and the properties of operations. Illustrate and **explain** the calculation by using equations, rectangular arrays, and/or area models.
	4.NBT.6	Find whole-number quotients and remainders with up to four-digit dividends and one-digit divisors, using strategies based on place value, the properties of operations, and/or the relationship between multiplication and division. Illustrate and **explain** the calculation by using equations, rectangular arrays, and/or area models.
Grade 5	**5.NBT.2**	**Explain** patterns in the number of zeros of the product when multiplying a number by powers of 10, and **explain** patterns in the placement of the decimal point when a decimal is multiplied or divided by a power of 10. Use whole-number exponents to denote powers of 10.
	5.NBT.6	Find whole-number quotients of whole numbers with up to four-digit dividends and two-digit divisors, using strategies based on place value, the properties of operations, and/or the relationship between multiplication and division. Illustrate and **explain** the calculation by using equations, rectangular arrays, and/or area models.
	5.NBT.7	Add, subtract, multiply, and divide decimals to hundredths, using concrete models or drawings and strategies based on place value, properties of operations, and/or the relationship between addition and subtraction; relate the strategy to a written method and **explain the reasoning used.**

Number and Operations—Fractions

Grade 3	**3.NF.3b,d**	**Explain** equivalence of fractions in special cases, and compare fractions by reasoning about their size. b. Recognize and generate simple equivalent fractions (e.g., 1/2 = 2/4, 4/6 = 2/3). **Explain why** the fractions are equivalent, e.g., by using a visual fraction model. d. Compare two fractions with the same numerator or the same denominator by reasoning about their size. Recognize that comparisons are valid only when the two fractions refer to the same whole. Record the results of comparisons with the symbols >, =, or <, and **justify the conclusions**, e.g., by using a visual fraction model.

K–8 Verbal Explanations, Verbal Descriptions, Explaining, Justifying
(continued)

Number and Operations—Fractions (continued)

Grade 4	4.NF.1	**Explain why** a fraction a/b is equivalent to a fraction $(n \times a)/(n \times b)$ by using visual fraction models, with attention to how the number and size of the parts differ even though the two fractions themselves are the same size. Use this principle to recognize and generate equivalent fractions.
	4.NF.2	Compare two fractions with different numerators and different denominators, e.g., by creating common denominators or numerators, or by comparing to a benchmark fraction such as 1/2. Recognize that comparisons are valid only when the two fractions refer to the same whole. Record the results of comparisons with symbols >, =, or <, and **justify the conclusions**, e.g., by using a visual fraction model.
	4.NF.3b	b. Decompose a fraction into a sum of fractions with the same denominator in more than one way, recording each decomposition by an equation. **Justify** decompositions, e.g., by using a visual fraction model. *Examples: 3/8 = 1/8 + 1/8 + 1/8 ; 3/8 = 1/8 + 2/8 ; 2 1/8 = 1 + 1 + 1/8 = 8/8 + 8/8 + 1/8.*
	4.NF.7	Compare two decimals to hundredths by reasoning about their size. Recognize that comparisons are valid only when the two decimals refer to the same whole. Record the results of comparisons with the symbols >, =, or <, and **justify the conclusions**, e.g., by using a visual model.
Grade 5	5.NF.5b	Interpret multiplication as scaling (resizing), by:
		b. **Explaining why** multiplying a given number by a fraction greater than 1 results in a product greater than the given number (recognizing multiplication by whole numbers greater than 1 as a familiar case); **explaining why** multiplying a given number by a fraction less than 1 results in a product smaller than the given number; and relating the principle of fraction equivalence $a/b = (n \times a)/(n \times b)$ to the effect of multiplying a/b by 1.

Measurement and Data

Kindergarten	K.MD.1	**Describe** measurable attributes of objects, such as length or weight. **Describe** several measurable attributes of a single object.
	K.MD.2	Directly compare two objects with a measurable attribute in common, to see which object has "more of"/"less of" the attribute, and **describe** the difference. *For example, directly compare the heights of two children and describe one child as taller/shorter.*

K–8 Verbal Explanations, Verbal Descriptions, Explaining, Justifying
(continued)

Measurement and Data *(continued)*

Grade 1	**1.MD.3**	**Tell** and write time in hours and half-hours using analog and digital clocks.
	1.MD.4	Organize, represent, and interpret data with up to three categories; **ask and answer** questions about the total number of data points, how many in each category, and how many more or less are in one category than in another.
	2.MD.2	Measure the length of an object twice, using length units of different lengths for the two measurements; **describe** how the two measurements relate to the size of the unit chosen.

Geometry

Kindergarten	**K.G.1**	**Describe** objects in the environment using names of shapes, and **describe** the relative positions of these objects using terms such as *above, below, beside, in front of, behind,* and *next to.*
	K.G.2	Correctly **name** shapes regardless of their orientations or overall size.
	K.G.4	Analyze and compare two- and three-dimensional shapes, in different sizes and orientations, using informal language to **describe** their similarities, differences, parts (e.g., number of sides and vertices/"corners") and other attributes (e.g., having sides of equal length).
Grade 1	**1.G.3**	Partition circles and rectangles into two and four equal shares, **describe** the shares using the words *halves, fourths,* and *quarters,* and use the phrases *half of, fourth of,* and *quarter of.* **Describe** the whole as two of, or four of the shares. Understand for these examples that decomposing into more equal shares creates smaller shares.
Grade 2	**2.G.3**	Partition circles and rectangles into two, three, or four equal shares, **describe** the shares using the words *halves, thirds, half of, a third of,* etc., and **describe** the whole as two halves, three thirds, four fourths. Recognize that equal shares of identical wholes need not have the same shape.
Grade 7	**7.G.3**	**Describe** the two-dimensional figures that result from slicing three-dimensional figures, as in plane sections of right rectangular prisms and right rectangular pyramids.

K–8 Verbal Explanations, Verbal Descriptions, Explaining, Justifying
(continued)

Geometry *(continued)*

Grade 8	**8.G.2**	Understand that a two-dimensional figure is congruent to another if the second can be obtained from the first by a sequence of rotations, reflections, and translations; given two congruent figures, **describe** a sequence that exhibits the congruence between them.
	8.G.3	**Describe** the effect of dilations, translations, rotations, and reflections on two-dimensional figures using coordinates.
	8.G.4	Understand that a two-dimensional figure is similar to another if the second can be obtained from the first by a sequence of rotations, reflections, translations, and dilations; given two similar two-dimensional figures, **describe** a sequence that exhibits the similarity between them.
	8.G.5	**Use informal arguments** to establish facts about the angle sum and exterior angle of triangles, about the angles created when parallel lines are cut by a transversal, and the angle-angle criterion for similarity of triangles. *For example, arrange three copies of the same triangle so that the sum of the three angles appears to form a line, and give an argument in terms of transversals why this is so.*
	8.G.6	**Explain** a proof of the Pythagorean Theorem and its converse.

Ratios and Proportional Relationships

Grade 6	**6.RP.1**	Understand the concept of a ratio and use ratio language to **describe** a ratio relationship between two quantities. *For example, "The ratio of wings to beaks in the bird house at the zoo was 2:1, because for every 2 wings there was 1 beak." "For every vote candidate A received, candidate C received nearly three votes."*
Grade 7	**7.RP.2b,d**	b. Identify the constant of proportionality (unit rate) in tables, graphs, equations, diagrams, and **verbal descriptions** of proportional relationships. d. **Explain** what a point (x, y) on the graph of a proportional relationship means in terms of the situation, with special attention to the points $(0, 0)$ and $(1, r)$ where r is the unit rate.

K–8 Verbal Explanations, Verbal Descriptions, Explaining, Justifying
(continued)

The Number System

Grade 6	**6.NS.5**	Understand that positive and negative numbers are used together to describe quantities having opposite directions or values (e.g., temperature above/below zero, elevation above/below sea level, credits/debits, positive/negative electric charge); use positive and negative numbers to represent quantities in real-world contexts, **explaining** the meaning of 0 in each situation.
	6.NS.7b	b. Write, interpret, and **explain** statements of order for rational numbers in real-world contexts. *For example, write −3°C > −7°C to express the fact that −3°C is warmer than −7°C.*
Grade 7	**7.NS.1a,b**	**a. Describe** situations in which opposite quantities combine to make 0. *For example, a hydrogen atom has 0 charge because its two constituents are oppositely charged.* b. Understand $p + q$ as the number located a distance $|q|$ from p, in the positive or negative direction depending on whether q is positive or negative. Show that a number and its opposite have a sum of 0 (are additive inverses). Interpret sums of rational numbers by **describing** real-world contexts.
	7.NS.2a,b	a. Understand that multiplication is extended from fractions to rational numbers by requiring that operations continue to satisfy the properties of operations, particularly the distributive property, leading to products such as $(-1)(-1) = 1$ and the rules for multiplying signed numbers. Interpret products of rational numbers by **describing** real-world contexts. b. Understand that integers can be divided, provided that the divisor is not zero, and every quotient of integers (with non-zero divisor) is a rational number. If p and q are integers, then $-(p/q) = (-p)/q = p/(-q)$. Interpret quotients of rational numbers by **describing** real-world contexts.

Expressions and Equations

Grade 8	**8.EE.6**	Use similar triangles to **explain** why the slope m is the same between any two distinct points on a non-vertical line in the coordinate plane; derive the equation y = mx for a line through the origin and the equation $y = mx + b$ for a line intercepting the vertical axis at b.

K–8 Verbal Explanations, Verbal Descriptions, Explaining, Justifying
(continued)

Functions

Grade 8	**8.F.2**	Compare properties of two functions each represented in a different way (algebraically, graphically, numerically in tables, or by **verbal descriptions**). *For example, given a linear function represented by a table of values and a linear function represented by an algebraic expression, determine which function has the greater rate of change.*
	8.F.5	**Describe** qualitatively the functional relationship between two quantities by analyzing a graph (e.g., where the function is increasing or decreasing, linear or nonlinear). Sketch a graph that exhibits the qualitative features of a function that has been **described verbally.**

Statistics and Probability

Grade 6	**6.SP.5b,c**	Summarize numerical data sets in relation to their context, such as by: b. **Describing** the nature of the attribute under investigation, including how it was measured and its units of measurement. c. Giving quantitative measures of center (median and/or mean) and variability (interquartile range and/or mean absolute deviation), as well as **describing** any overall pattern and any striking deviations from the overall pattern with reference to the context in which the data were gathered.
Grade 7	**7.SP.7**	Develop a probability model and use it to find probabilities of events. Compare probabilities from a model to observed frequencies; if the agreement is not good, **explain** possible sources of the discrepancy.
Grade 8	**8.SP.1**	Construct and interpret scatter plots for bivariate measurement data to investigate patterns of association between two quantities. **Describe** patterns such as clustering, outliers, positive or negative association, linear association, and nonlinear association.
	8.SP.4	Understand that patterns of association can also be seen in bivariate categorical data by displaying frequencies and relative frequencies in a two-way table. Construct and interpret a two-way table summarizing data on two categorical variables collected from the same subjects. Use relative frequencies calculated for rows or columns to **describe** possible association between the two variables. *For example, collect data from students in your class on whether or not they have a curfew on school nights and whether or not they have assigned chores at home. Is there evidence that those who have a curfew also tend to have chores?*

Source: Common Core State Standards for Mathematics (CCSSI, 2010).

K–8 Solving Word Problems

Operations and Algebraic Thinking

Kindergarten	**K.OA.2**	**Solve** addition and subtraction **word problems**, and add and subtract within 10, e.g., by using objects or drawings to represent the problem.
Grade 1	**1.OA.1**	Use addition and subtraction within 20 to **solve word problems** involving situations of adding to, taking from, putting together, taking apart, and comparing, with unknowns in all positions, e.g., by using objects, drawings, and equations with a symbol for the unknown number to represent the problem.
	1.OA.2	**Solve word problems** that call for addition of three whole numbers whose sum is less than or equal to 20, e.g., by using objects, drawings, and equations with a symbol for the unknown number to represent the problem.
Grade 2	**2.OA.1**	Use addition and subtraction within 100 to **solve one- and two-step word problems** involving situations of adding to, taking from, putting together, taking apart, and comparing, with unknowns in all positions, e.g., by using drawings and equations with a symbol for the unknown number to represent the problem.
Grade 3	**3.OA.3**	Use multiplication and division within 100 to **solve word problems** in situations involving equal groups, arrays, and measurement quantities, e.g., by using drawings and equations with a symbol for the unknown number to represent the problem.
	3.OA.8	**Solve two-step word problems** using the four operations. Represent these problems using equations with a letter standing for the unknown quantity. Assess the reasonableness of answers using mental computation and estimation strategies including rounding.
Grade 4	**4.OA.2**	Multiply or divide to **solve word problems** involving multiplicative comparison, e.g., by using drawings and equations with a symbol for the unknown number to represent the problem, distinguishing multiplicative comparison from additive comparison.
	4.OA.3	**Solve multistep word problems** posed with whole numbers and having whole-number answers using the four operations, including problems in which remainders must be interpreted. Represent these problems using equations with a letter standing for the unknown quantity. Assess the reasonableness of answers using mental computation and estimation strategies including rounding.

K–8 Solving Word Problems *(continued)*

Measurement and Data

Grade 2	**2.MD.5**	Use addition and subtraction within 100 to **solve word problems** involving lengths that are given in the same units, e.g., by using drawings (such as drawings of rulers) and equations with a symbol for the unknown number to represent the problem.
	2.MD.8	**Solve word problems** involving dollar bills, quarters, dimes, nickels, and pennies, using $ and ¢ symbols appropriately. Example: If you have 2 dimes and 3 pennies, how many cents do you have?
Grade 3	**3.MD.1**	Tell and write time to the nearest minute and measure time intervals in minutes. **Solve word problems** involving addition and subtraction of time intervals in minutes, e.g., by representing the problem on a number line diagram.
	3.MD.2	Measure and estimate liquid volumes and masses of objects using standard units of grams (g), kilograms (kg), and liters (l). Add, subtract, multiply, or divide to **solve one-step word problems** involving masses or volumes that are given in the same units, e.g., by using drawings (such as a beaker with a measurement scale) to represent the problem.
Grade 4	**4.MD.2**	Use the four operations to **solve word problems** involving distances, intervals of time, liquid volumes, masses of objects, and money, including problems involving simple fractions or decimals, and problems that require expressing measurements given in a larger unit in terms of a smaller unit. Represent measurement quantities using diagrams such as number line diagrams that feature a measurement scale.

K–8 Solving Word Problems *(continued)*

Number and Operations—Fractions

Grade 4	**4.NF.3d**	d. **Solve word problems** involving addition and subtraction of fractions referring to the same whole and having like denominators, e.g., by using visual fraction models and equations to represent the problem.
	4.NF.4c	c. **Solve word problems** involving multiplication of a fraction by a whole number, e.g., by using visual fraction models and equations to represent the problem. *For example, if each person at a party will eat 3/8 of a pound of roast beef, and there will be 5 people at the party, how many pounds of roast beef will be needed? Between what two whole numbers does your answer lie?*
Grade 5	**5.NF.2**	**Solve word problems** involving addition and subtraction of fractions referring to the same whole, including cases of unlike denominators, e.g., by using visual fraction models or equations to represent the problem. Use benchmark fractions and number sense of fractions to estimate mentally and assess the reasonableness of answers. *For example, recognize an incorrect result 2/5 + 1/2 = 3/7, by observing that 3/7 < 1/2.*
	5.NF.3	Interpret a fraction as division of the numerator by the denominator (a/b = a ÷ b). **Solve word problems** involving division of whole numbers leading to answers in the form of fractions or mixed numbers, e.g., by using visual fraction models or equations to represent the problem. *For example, interpret 3/4 as the result of dividing 3 by 4, noting that 3/4 multiplied by 4 equals 3, and that when 3 wholes are shared equally among 4 people each person has a share of size 3/4. If 9 people want to share a 50-pound sack of rice equally by weight, how many pounds of rice should each person get? Between what two whole numbers does your answer lie?*

K–8 Solving Word Problems *(continued)*

The Number System

Grade 6	**6.NS.1**	Interpret and compute quotients of fractions, and **solve word problems** involving division of fractions by fractions, e.g., by using visual fraction models and equations to represent the problem. *For example, create a story context for (2/3) ÷ (3/4) and use a visual fraction model to show the quotient; use the relationship between multiplication and division to explain that (2/3) ÷ (3/4) = 8/9 because 3/4 of 8/9 is 2/3. (In general, (a/b) ÷ (c/d) = ad/bc.) How much chocolate will each person get if 3 people share 1/2 lb of chocolate equally? How many 3/4-cup servings are in 2/3 of a cup of yogurt? How wide is a rectangular strip of land with length 3/4 mi and area 1/2 square mi?*

Expressions and Equations

Grade 7	**7.EE.4a,b**	Use variables to represent quantities in a real-world or mathematical problem, and construct simple equations and inequalities to solve problems by reasoning about the quantities. a. **Solve word problems** leading to equations of the form $px + q = r$ and $p(x + q) = r$, where p, q, and r are specific rational numbers. Solve equations of these forms fluently. Compare an algebraic solution to an arithmetic solution, identifying the sequence of the operations used in each approach. *For example, the perimeter of a rectangle is 54 cm. Its length is 6 cm. What is its width?* b. **Solve word problems** leading to inequalities of the form $px + q > r$ or $px + q < r$, where p, q, and r are specific rational numbers. Graph the solution set of the inequality and interpret it in the context of the problem. *For example: As a salesperson, you are paid $50 per week plus $3 per sale. This week you want your pay to be at least $100. Write an inequality for the number of sales you need to make, and describe the solutions.*

Source: Common Core State Standards for Mathematics (CCSSI, 2010).

K–8 Solving Real-World and Mathematical Problems

Number and Operations—Fractions

Grade 5	**5.NF.6**	**Solve real-world problems** involving multiplication of fractions and mixed numbers, e.g., by using visual fraction models or equations to represent the problem.
	5.NF.7c	c. **Solve real-world problems** involving division of unit fractions by non-zero whole numbers and division of whole numbers by unit fractions, e.g., by using visual fraction models and equations to represent the problem. *For example, how much chocolate will each person get if 3 people share 1/2 lb of chocolate equally? How many 1/3-cup servings are in 2 cups of raisins?*

The Number System

Grade 6	**6.NS.5**	Understand that positive and negative numbers are used together to describe quantities having opposite directions or values (e.g., temperature above/below zero, elevation above/below sea level, credits/debits, positive/negative electric charge); use positive and negative numbers to represent quantities in **real-world contexts**, explaining the meaning of 0 in each situation.
	6.NS.7b,c	b. Write, interpret, and explain statements of order for rational numbers in **real-world contexts.** *For example, write –3 °C > –7 °C to express the fact that –3 °C is warmer than –7 °C.* c. Understand the absolute value of a rational number as its distance from 0 on the number line; interpret absolute value as magnitude for a positive or negative quantity in a **real-world situation.** *For example, for an account balance of –30 dollars, write |–30| = 30 to describe the size of the debt in dollars.*
	6.NS.8	**Solve real-world and mathematical problems** by graphing points in all four quadrants of the coordinate plane. Include use of coordinates and absolute value to find distances between points with the same first coordinate or the same second coordinate.

K–8 Solving Real-World and Mathematical Problems *(continued)*

The Number System *(continued)*

Grade 7	**7.NS.1b,c**	b. Understand $p + q$ as the number located a distance $|q|$ from p, in the positive or negative direction depending on whether q is positive or negative. Show that a number and its opposite have a sum of 0 (are additive inverses). Interpret sums of rational numbers by describing **real-world contexts.** c. Understand subtraction of rational numbers as adding the additive inverse, $p - q = p + (-q)$. Show that the distance between two rational numbers on the number line is the absolute value of their difference, and apply this principle in **real-world contexts.**
	7.NS.2a,b	a. Understand that multiplication is extended from fractions to rational numbers by requiring that operations continue to satisfy the properties of operations, particularly the distributive property, leading to products such as $(-1)(-1) = 1$ and the rules for multiplying signed numbers. Interpret products of rational numbers by describing **real-world contexts**. b. Understand that integers can be divided, provided that the divisor is not zero, and every quotient of integers (with non-zero divisor) is a rational number. If p and q are integers, then $-(p/q) = (-p)/q = p/(-q)$. Interpret quotients of rational numbers by describing **real-world contexts.**
	7.NS.3	**Solve real-world and mathematical problems** involving the four operations with rational numbers.

K–8 Solving Real-World and Mathematical Problems *(continued)*

Measurement and Data

Grade 3	**3.MD.7b,d**	Relate area to the operations of multiplication and addition. b. Multiply side lengths to find areas of rectangles with whole-number side lengths in the context of **solving real-world and mathematical problems,** and represent whole-number products as rectangular areas in mathematical reasoning. d. Recognize area as additive. Find areas of rectilinear figures by decomposing them into non-overlapping rectangles and adding the areas of the non-overlapping parts, applying this technique to **solve real-world problems**.
	3.MD.8	**Solve real-world and mathematical problems** involving perimeters of polygons, including finding the perimeter given the side lengths, finding an unknown side length, and exhibiting rectangles with the same perimeter and different areas or with the same area and different perimeters.
Grade 4	**4.MD.3**	Apply area and perimeter formulas for rectangles in **real-world and mathematical problems.** *For example, find the width of a rectangular room given the area of the flooring and the length, by viewing the area formula as a multiplication equation with an unknown factor.*
	4.MD.7	Recognize angle measure as additive. When an angle is decomposed into non-overlapping parts, the angle measure of the whole is the sum of the angle measures of the parts. **Solve** addition and subtraction problems to find unknown angles on a diagram in **real-world and mathematical problems**, e.g., by using an equation with a symbol for the unknown angle measure.
Grade 5	**5.MD.5b,c**	Relate volume to the operations of multiplication and addition and **solve real-world and mathematical problems** involving volume. b. Apply the formulas $V = l \times w \times h$ and $V = b \times h$ for rectangular prisms to find volumes of right rectangular prisms with whole-number edge lengths in the context of **solving real-world and mathematical problems**. c. Recognize volume as additive. Find volumes of solid figures composed of two non-overlapping right rectangular prisms by adding the volumes of the non-overlapping parts, applying this technique to **solve real-world problems**.

K–8 Solving Real-World and Mathematical Problems *(continued)*

Geometry

Grade 5	**5.G.2**	Represent **real-world and mathematical problems** by graphing points in the first quadrant of the coordinate plane, and interpret coordinate values of points in the context of the situation.
Grade 6	**6.G.1**	Find the area of right triangles, other triangles, special quadrilaterals, and polygons by composing into rectangles or decomposing into triangles and other shapes; apply these techniques in the context of **solving real-world and mathematical problems.**.
	6.G.2	Find the volume of a right rectangular prism with fractional edge lengths by packing it with unit cubes of the appropriate unit fraction edge lengths, and show that the volume is the same as would be found by multiplying the edge lengths of the prism. Apply the formula $V = l\,w\,h$ and $V\,b\,h$ to find volumes of right rectangular prisms with fractional edge lengths in the context of **solving real-world and mathematical problems**.
	6.G.3	Draw polygons in the coordinate plane given coordinates for the vertices; use coordinates to find the length of a side joining points with the same first coordinate or the same second coordinate. Apply these techniques in the context of **solving real-world and mathematical problems**.
	6.G.4	Represent three-dimensional figures using nets made up of rectangles and triangles, and using the nets to find the surface area of these figures. Apply these techniques in the context of **solving real-world and mathematical problems**.
Grade 7	**7.G.6**	**Solve real-world and mathematical problems** involving area, volume and surface area of two- and three-dimensional objects composed of triangles, quadrilaterals, polygons, cubes, and right prisms.
Grade 8	**8.G.7**	Apply the Pythagorean Theorem to determine unknown side lengths in right triangles in **real-world and mathematical problems** in two and three dimensions.
	8.G.9	Know the formulas for the volumes of cones, cylinders, and spheres and use them to **solve real-world and mathematical problems**.

K–8 Solving Real-World and Mathematical Problems *(continued)*

Ratios and Proportional Relationships

Grade 6	6.RP.3a,b,c,d	Use ratio and rate reasoning to solve **real-world and mathematical problems**, e.g., by reasoning about tables of equivalent ratios, tape diagrams, double number line diagrams, or equations. a. Make tables of equivalent ratios relating quantities with whole-number measurements, find missing values in the tables, and plot the pairs of values on the coordinate plane. Use tables to compare ratios. b. Solve unit rate problems including those involving unit pricing and constant speed. *For example, if it took 7 hours to mow 4 lawns, then at that rate, how many lawns could be mowed in 35 hours? At what rate were lawns being mowed?* c. Find a percent of a quantity as a rate per 100 (e.g., 30% of a quantity means 30/100 times the quantity); solve problems involving finding the whole, given a part and the percent. d. Use ratio reasoning to convert measurement units; manipulate and transform units appropriately when multiplying or dividing quantities.

Expressions and Equations

Grade 6	6.EE.2c	c. Evaluate expressions at specific values of their variables. Include expressions that arise from formulas used in **real-world problems**. Perform arithmetic operations, including those involving whole-number exponents, in the conventional order when there are no parentheses to specify a particular order (Order of Operations). *For example, use the formulas $V = s^3$ and $A = 6 s^2$ to find the volume and surface area of a cube with sides of length $s = 1/2$.*
	6.EE.6	Use variables to represent numbers and write expressions when **solving a real-world or mathematical problem**; understand that a variable can represent an unknown number, or, depending on the purpose at hand, any number in a specified set.
	6.EE.7	**Solve real-world and mathematical problems** by writing and solving equations of the form $x + p = q$ and $px = q$ for cases in which p, q, and x are all nonnegative rational numbers.
	6.EE.8	Write an inequality of the form $x > c$ or $x < c$ to represent a constraint or condition in a **real-world or mathematical problem**. Recognize that inequalities of the form $x > c$ or $x < c$ have infinitely many solutions; represent solutions of such inequalities on number line diagrams.

K–8 Solving Real-World and Mathematical Problems *(continued)*

Expressions and Equations *(continued)*

Grade 6	**6.EE.9**	Use variables to represent two quantities in a **real-world problem** that change in relationship to one another; write an equation to express one quantity, thought of as the dependent variable, in terms of the other quantity, thought of as the independent variable. Analyze the relationship between the dependent and independent variables using graphs and tables, and relate these to the equation. *For example, in a problem involving motion at constant speed, list and graph ordered pairs of distances and times, and write the equation d = 65t to represent the relationship between distance and time.*
Grade 7	**7.EE.3**	**Solve multi-step real-life and mathematical problems** posed with positive and negative rational numbers in any form (whole numbers, fractions, and decimals), using tools strategically. Apply properties of operations to calculate with numbers in any form; convert between forms as appropriate; and assess the reasonableness of answers using mental computation and estimation strategies. *For example: If a woman making $25 an hour gets a 10% raise, she will make an additional 1/10 of her salary an hour, or $2.50, for a new salary of $27.50. If you want to place a towel bar 9 3/4 inches long in the center of a door that is 27 1/2 inches wide, you will need to place the bar about 9 inches from each edge; this estimate can be used as a check on the exact computation.*
	7.EE.4a,b	Use variables to represent quantities in a **real-world or mathematical problem**, and construct simple equations and inequalities to solve problems by reasoning about the quantities. a. Solve word problems leading to equations of the form $px + q = r$ and $p(x + q) = r$, where p, q, and r are specific rational numbers. Solve equations of these forms fluently. Compare an algebraic solution to an arithmetic solution, identifying the sequence of the operations used in each approach. *For example, the perimeter of a rectangle is 54 cm. Its length is 6 cm. What is its width?* b. Solve word problems leading to inequalities of the form $px + q > r$ or $px + q < r$, where p, q, and r are specific rational numbers. Graph the solution set of the inequality and interpret it in the context of the problem. *For example: As a salesperson, you are paid $50 per week plus $3 per sale. This week you want your pay to be at least $100. Write an inequality for the number of sales you need to make, and describe the solutions.*
Grade 8	**8.EE.8c**	c. **Solve real-world and mathematical problems** leading to two linear equations in two variables. *For example, given coordinates for two pairs of points, determine whether the line through the first pair of points intersects the line through the second pair.*

Source: Common Core State Standards for Mathematics (CCSSI, 2010).

Points of Intersection

> "The Standards for Mathematical Content are a balanced combination of procedure and understanding. Expectations that begin with the word **"understand"** are often especially good opportunities to connect the practices to the content."
>
> "In this respect, those content standards which set an expectation of **understanding** are potential 'points of intersection' between the Standards for Mathematical Content and the Standards for Mathematical Practice."
>
> —CCSSI, 2010, p. 8

Counting and Cardinality		
Kindergarten	**K.CC.4b,c**	**Understand** the relationship between numbers and quantities; connect counting to cardinality. b. **Understand** that the last number name said tells the number of objects counted. The number of objects is the same regardless of their arrangement or the order in which they were counted. c. **Understand** that each successive number name refers to a quantity that is one larger.

Operations and Algebraic Thinking		
Grade 1	**1.OA.4**	**Understand** subtraction as an unknown-addend problem. *For example, subtract 10 – 8 by finding the number that makes 10 when added to 8.*
	1.OA.7	**Understand** the meaning of the equal sign, and determine if equations involving addition and subtraction are true or false. *For example, which of the following equations are true and which are false? 6 = 6, 7 = 8 – 1, 5 + 2 = 2 + 5, 4 + 1 = 5 + 2.*
Grade 3	**3.OA.6**	**Understand** division as an unknown-factor problem. *For example, find 32 ÷ 8 by finding the number that makes 32 when multiplied by 8.*

Number and Operations in Base Ten		
Kindergarten	**K.NBT.1**	Compose and decompose numbers from 11 to 19 into ten ones and some further ones, e.g., by using objects or drawings, and record each composition or decomposition by a drawing or equation (such as 18 = 10 + 8); **understand** that these numbers are composed of ten ones and one, two, three, four, five, six, seven, eight, or nine ones.

Number and Operations in Base Ten *(continued)*		
Grade 1	**1.NBT.2a,b,c**	**Understand** that the two digits of a two-digit number represent amounts of tens and ones. **Understand** the following as special cases: a. 10 can be thought of as a bundle of ten ones — called a "ten." b. The numbers from 11 to 19 are composed of a ten and one, two, three, four, five, six, seven, eight, or nine ones. c. The numbers 10, 20, 30, 40, 50, 60, 70, 80, 90 refer to one, two, three, four, five, six, seven, eight, or nine tens (and 0 ones).
	1.NBT.4	Add within 100, including adding a two-digit number and a one-digit number, and adding a two-digit number and a multiple of 10, using concrete models or drawings and strategies based on place value, properties of operations, and/or the relationship between addition and subtraction; relate the strategy to a written method and explain the reasoning used. **Understand** that in adding two-digit numbers, one adds tens and tens, ones and ones; and sometimes it is necessary to compose a ten.
Grade 2	**2.NBT.1a,b**	**Understand** that the three digits of a three-digit number represent amounts of hundreds, tens, and ones; e.g., 706 equals 7 hundreds, 0 tens, and 6 ones. **Understand** the following as special cases: a. 100 can be thought of as a bundle of ten tens — called a "hundred." b. The numbers 100, 200, 300, 400, 500, 600, 700, 800, 900 refer to one, two, three, four, five, six, seven, eight, or nine hundreds (and 0 tens and 0 ones).
	2.NBT.7	Add and subtract within 1000, using concrete models or drawings and strategies based on place value, properties of operations, and/or the relationship between addition and subtraction; relate the strategy to a written method. **Understand** that in adding or subtracting three-digit numbers, one adds or subtracts hundreds and hundreds, tens and tens, ones and ones; and sometimes it is necessary to compose or decompose tens or hundreds.
Number and Operations—Fractions		
Grade 3	**3.NF.1**	**Understand** a fraction $1/b$ as the quantity formed by 1 part when a whole is partitioned into b equal parts; **understand** a fraction a/b as the quantity formed by a parts of size $1/b$.
	3.NF.2	**Understand** a fraction as a number on the number line; represent fractions on a number line diagram.
	3.NF.3a	a. **Understand** two fractions as equivalent (equal) if they are the same size, or the same point on a number line.

		Number and Operations—Fractions *(continued)*
Grade 4	**4.NF.3a**	**Understand** a fraction a/b with $a > 1$ as a sum of fractions $1/b$. a. **Understand** addition and subtraction of fractions as joining and separating parts referring to the same whole.
	4.NF.4a,b	a. **Understand** a fraction a/b as a multiple of $1/b$. *For example, use a visual fraction model to represent 5/4 as the product 5 × (1/4), recording the conclusion by the equation 5/4 = 5 × (1/4).* b. **Understand** a multiple of a/b as a multiple of $1/b$, and use this understanding to multiply a fraction by a whole number. *For example, use a visual fraction model to express 3 × (2/5) as 6 × (1/5), recognizing this product as 6/5. (In general, n × (a/b) = (n × a)/b.)*
		Measurement and Data
Grade 1	**1.MD.2**	Express the length of an object as a whole number of length units, by laying multiple copies of a shorter object (the length unit) end to end; **understand** that the length measurement of an object is the number of same-size length units that span it with no gaps or overlaps. *Limit to contexts where the object being measured is spanned by a whole number of length units with no gaps or overlaps.*
Grade 3	**3.MD.5**	Recognize area as an attribute of plane figures and **understand** concepts of area measurement.
Grade 4	**4.MD.5**	Recognize angles as geometric shapes that are formed wherever two rays share a common endpoint, and **understand** concepts of angle measurement.
Grade 5	**5.MD.3**	Recognize volume as an attribute of solid figures and **understand** concepts of volume measurement.
		Geometry
Grade 1	**1.G.3**	Partition circles and rectangles into two and four equal shares, describe the shares using the words *halves*, *fourths*, and *quarters*, and use the phrases *half of*, *fourth of*, and *quarter of*. Describe the whole as two of, or four of the shares. **Understand** for these examples that decomposing into more equal shares creates smaller shares.
Grade 3	**3.G.1**	**Understand** that shapes in different categories (e.g., rhombuses, rectangles, and others) may share attributes (e.g., having four sides), and that the shared attributes can define a larger category (e.g., quadrilaterals). Recognize rhombuses, rectangles, and squares as examples of quadrilaterals, and draw examples of quadrilaterals that do not belong to any of these subcategories.

Geometry *(continued)*		
Grade 5	5.G.1	Use a pair of perpendicular number lines, called axes, to define a coordinate system, with the intersection of the lines (the origin) arranged to coincide with the 0 on each line and a given point in the plane located by using an ordered pair of numbers, called its coordinates. **Understand** that the first number indicates how far to travel from the origin in the direction of one axis, and the second number indicates how far to travel in the direction of the second axis, with the convention that the names of the two axes and the coordinates correspond (e.g., x-axis and x-coordinate, y-axis and y-coordinate).
	5.G.3	**Understand** that attributes belonging to a category of two-dimensional figures also belong to all subcategories of that category. *For example, all rectangles have four right angles and squares are rectangles, so all squares have four right angles.*
Grade 8	8.G.2	**Understand** that a two-dimensional figure is congruent to another if the second can be obtained from the first by a sequence of rotations, reflections, and translations; given two congruent figures, describe a sequence that exhibits the congruence between them.
	8.G.4	**Understand** that a two-dimensional figure is similar to another if the second can be obtained from the first by a sequence of rotations, reflections, translations, and dilations; given two similar two-dimensional figures, describe a sequence that exhibits the similarity between them.
Ratios and Proportional Reasoning		
Grade 6	6.RP.1	**Understand** the concept of a ratio and use ratio language to describe a ratio relationship between two quantities. *For example, "The ratio of wings to beaks in the bird house at the zoo was 2:1, because for every 2 wings there was 1 beak." "For every vote candidate A received, candidate C received nearly three votes."*
	6.RP.2	**Understand** the concept of a unit rate a/b associated with a ratio $a:b$ with $b \neq 0$, and use rate language in the context of a ratio relationship. *For example, "This recipe has a ratio of 3 cups of flour to 4 cups of sugar, so there is 3/4 cup of flour for each cup of sugar." "We paid $75 for 15 hamburgers, which is a rate of $5 per hamburger."*

The Number Systems		
Grade 6	**6.NS.5**	**Understand** that positive and negative numbers are used together to describe quantities having opposite directions or values (e.g., temperature above/below zero, elevation above/below sea level, credits/debits, positive/negative electric charge); use positive and negative numbers to represent quantities in real-world contexts, explaining the meaning of 0 in each situation.
	6.NS.6b	**Understand** a rational number as a point on the number line. Extend number line diagrams and coordinate axes familiar from previous grades to represent points on the line and in the plane with negative number coordinates. b. **Understand** signs of numbers in ordered pairs as indicating locations in quadrants of the coordinate plane; recognize that when two ordered pairs differ only by signs, the locations of the points are related by reflections across one or both axes.
	6.NS.7c	**Understand** ordering and absolute value of rational numbers. c. **Understand** the absolute value of a rational number as its distance from 0 on the number line; interpret absolute value as magnitude for a positive or negative quantity in a real-world situation. *For example, for an account balance of −30 dollars, write $|−30| = 30$ to describe the size of the debt in dollars.*
Grade 7	**7.NS.1b,c**	b. **Understand** $p + q$ as the number located a distance $|q|$ from p, in the positive or negative direction depending on whether q is positive or negative. Show that a number and its opposite have a sum of 0 (are additive inverses). Interpret sums of rational numbers by describing real-world contexts. c. **Understand** subtraction of rational numbers as adding the additive inverse, $p − q = p + (−q)$. Show that the distance between two rational numbers on the number line is the absolute value of their difference, and apply this principle in real-world contexts.
	7.NS.2a,b	a. **Understand** that multiplication is extended from fractions to rational numbers by requiring that operations continue to satisfy the properties of operations, particularly the distributive property, leading to products such as $(−1)(−1) = 1$ and the rules for multiplying signed numbers. Interpret products of rational numbers by describing real-world contexts. b. **Understand** that integers can be divided, provided that the divisor is not zero, and every quotient of integers (with non-zero divisor) is a rational number. If p and q are integers, then $−(p/q) = (−p)/q = p/(−q)$. Interpret quotients of rational numbers by describing real-world contexts.
Grade 8	**8.NS.1**	Know that numbers that are not rational are called irrational. **Understand** informally that every number has a decimal expansion; for rational numbers show that the decimal expansion repeats eventually, and convert a decimal expansion which repeats eventually into a rational number.

Expressions and Equations		
Grade 6	6.EE.5	**Understand** solving an equation or inequality as a process of answering a question: which values from a specified set, if any, make the equation or inequality true? Use substitution to determine whether a given number in a specified set makes an equation or inequality true.
	6.EE.6	Use variables to represent numbers and write expressions when solving a real-world or mathematical problem; **understand** that a variable can represent an unknown number, or, depending on the purpose at hand, any number in a specified set.
Grade 7	7.EE.2	**Understand** that rewriting an expression in different forms in a problem context can shed light on the problem and how the quantities in it are related. *For example, a + 0.05a = 1.05a means that "increase by 5%" is the same as "multiply by 1.05."*
Grade 8	8.EE.8a	a. **Understand** that solutions to a system of two linear equations in two variables correspond to points of intersection of their graphs, because points of intersection satisfy both equations simultaneously.
Statistics and Probability		
Grade 6	6.SP.2	**Understand** that a set of data collected to answer a statistical question has a distribution which can be described by its center, spread, and overall shape.
Grade 7	7.SP.1	**Understand** that statistics can be used to gain information about a population by examining a sample of the population; generalizations about a population from a sample are valid only if the sample is representative of that population. **Understand** that random sampling tends to produce representative samples and support valid inferences.
	7.SP.5	**Understand** that the probability of a chance event is a number between 0 and 1 that expresses the likelihood of the event occurring. Larger numbers indicate greater likelihood. A probability near 0 indicates an unlikely event, a probability around 1/2 indicates an event that is neither unlikely nor likely, and a probability near 1 indicates a likely event.
	7.SP.8a	a. **Understand** that, just as with simple events, the probability of a compound event is the fraction of outcomes in the sample space for which the compound event occurs.
Grade 8	8.SP.4	**Understand** that patterns of association can also be seen in bivariate categorical data by displaying frequencies and relative frequencies in a two-way table. Construct and interpret a two-way table summarizing data on two categorical variables collected from the same subjects. Use relative frequencies calculated for rows or columns to describe possible association between the two variables. *For example, collect data from students in your class on whether or not they have a curfew on school nights and whether or not they have assigned chores at home. Is there evidence that those who have a curfew also tend to have chores?*

Functions		
Grade 8	**8.F.1**	**Understand** that a function is a rule that assigns to each input exactly one output. The graph of a function is the set of ordered pairs consisting of an input and the corresponding output.

Number and Quantity		
High School	**N-VM.4a,c**	(+) Add and subtract vectors. a. Add vectors end-to-end, component-wise, and by the parallelogram rule. **Understand** that the magnitude of a sum of two vectors is typically not the sum of the magnitudes. c. **Understand** vector subtraction $v - w$ as $v + (-w)$, where $-w$ is the additive inverse of w, with the same magnitude as w and pointing in the opposite direction. Represent vector subtraction graphically by connecting the tips in the appropriate order, and perform vector subtraction component-wise.
	N-VM.9	(+) **Understand** that, unlike multiplication of numbers, matrix multiplication for square matrices is not a commutative operation, but still satisfies the associative and distributive properties.
	N-VM.10	(+) **Understand** that the zero and identity matrices play a role in matrix addition and multiplication similar to the role of 0 and 1 in the real numbers. The determinant of a square matrix is nonzero if and only if the matrix has a multiplicative inverse.

Algebra		
High School	**A-APR.1**	**Understand** that polynomials form a system analogous to the integers, namely, they are closed under the operations of addition, subtraction, and multiplication; add, subtract, and multiply polynomials.
	A-APR.7	(+) **Understand** that rational expressions form a system analogous to the rational numbers, closed under addition, subtraction, multiplication, and division by a nonzero rational expression; add, subtract, multiply, and divide rational expressions.
	A-REI.10	**Understand** that the graph of an equation in two variables is the set of all its solutions plotted in the coordinate plane, often forming a curve (which could be a line).

Functions		
High School	**F-IF.1**	**Understand** that a function from one set (called the domain) to another set (called the range) assigns to each element of the domain exactly one element of the range. If f is a function and x is an element of its domain, then $f(x)$ denotes the output of f corresponding to the input x. The graph of f is the graph of the equation $y = f(x)$.
	F-BF.5	(+) **Understand** the inverse relationship between exponents and logarithms and use this relationship to solve problems involving logarithms and exponents.
	F-TF.1	**Understand** radian measure of an angle as the length of the arc on the unit circle subtended by the angle.
	F-TF.6	(+) **Understand** that restricting a trigonometric function to a domain on which it is always increasing or always decreasing allows its inverse to be constructed.
Geometry		
High School	**G-SRT.6**	**Understand** that by similarity, side ratios in right triangles are properties of the angles in the triangle, leading to definitions of trigonometric ratios for acute angles.
	G-SRT.11	(+) **Understand** and apply the Law of Sines and the Law of Cosines to find unknown measurements in right and non-right triangles (e.g., surveying problems, resultant forces).
Statistics and Probability		
High School	**S-IC.1**	**Understand** statistics as a process for making inferences about population parameters based on a random sample from that population.
	S-CP.2	**Understand** that two events A and B are independent if the probability of A and B occurring together is the product of their probabilities, and use this characterization to determine if they are independent.
	S-CP.3	**Understand** the conditional probability of A given B as $P(A \text{ and } B)/P(B)$, and interpret independence of A and B as saying that the conditional probability of A given B is the same as the probability of A, and the conditional probability of B given A is the same as the probability of B.

Source: Common Core State Standards for Mathematics (CCSSI, 2010).

APPENDIX D

High School
Modeling Standards

> "Modeling is best interpreted not as a collection of isolated topics but in relation to other standards. Making mathematical models is a Standard for Mathematical Practice, and specific modeling standards appear throughout the high school standards indicated by a star symbol (*). The star symbol sometimes appears on the heading for a group of standards; in that case, it should be understood to apply to all standards in that group."
>
> —CCSSI, 2010, p. 57

Algebra		
High School	**A-SSE.1a,b**	Interpret expressions that represent a quantity in terms of its context.* a. Interpret parts of an expression, such as terms, factors, and coefficients. b. Interpret complicated expressions by viewing one or more of their parts as a single entity. *For example, interpret $P(1+r)^n$ as the product of P and a factor not depending on P.*
	A-SSE.3a,b,c	Choose and produce an equivalent form of an expression to reveal and explain properties of the quantity represented by the expression.* a. Factor a quadratic expression to reveal the zeros of the function it defines. b. Complete the square in a quadratic expression to reveal the maximum or minimum value of the function it defines. c. Use the properties of exponents to transform expressions for exponential functions. *For example, the expression 1.15^t can be rewritten as $(1.15^{1/12})^{12t} \approx 1.012^{12t}$ to reveal the approximate equivalent monthly interest rate if the annual rate is 15%.*
	A-SSE.4	Derive the formula for the sum of a finite geometric series (when the common ratio is not 1), and use the formula to solve problems. *For example, calculate mortgage payments.**
	A-REI.11	Explain why the x-coordinates of the points where the graphs of the equations $y = f(x)$ and $y = g(x)$ intersect are the solutions of the equation $f(x) = g(x)$; find the solutions approximately, e.g., using technology to graph the functions, make tables of values, or find successive approximations. Include cases where $f(x)$ and/or $g(x)$ are linear, polynomial, rational, absolute value, exponential, and logarithmic functions.*

		Functions
High School	**F-IF.4**	For a function that models a relationship between two quantities, interpret key features of graphs and tables in terms of the quantities, and sketch graphs showing key features given a verbal description of the relationship. *Key features include: intercepts; intervals where the function is increasing, decreasing, positive, or negative; relative maximums and minimums; symmetries; end behavior; and periodicity.*★
	F-IF.5	Relate the domain of a function to its graph and, where applicable, to the quantitative relationship it describes. *For example, if the function h(n) gives the number of person-hours it takes to assemble n engines in a factory, then the positive integers would be an appropriate domain for the function.*★
	F-IF.6	Calculate and interpret the average rate of change of a function (presented symbolically or as a table) over a specified interval. Estimate the rate of change from a graph.★
	F-IF.7a,b,c,d,e	Graph functions expressed symbolically and show key features of the graph, by hand in simple cases and using technology for more complicated cases.★
		a. Graph linear and quadratic functions and show intercepts, maxima, and minima.
		b. Graph square root, cube root, and piecewise-defined functions, including step functions and absolute value functions.
		c. Graph polynomial functions, identifying zeros when suitable factorizations are available, and showing end behavior.
		d. (+) Graph rational functions, identifying zeros and asymptotes when suitable factorizations are available, and showing end behavior.
		e. Graph exponential and logarithmic functions, showing intercepts and end behavior, and trigonometric functions, showing period, midline, and amplitude.
	F-BF.1a,b,c	Write a function that describes a relationship between two quantities.★
		a. Determine an explicit expression, a recursive process, or steps for calculation from a context.
		b. Combine standard function types using arithmetic operations. *For example, build a function that models the temperature of a cooling body by adding a constant function to a decaying exponential, and relate these functions to the model.*
		c. (+) Compose functions. *For example, if T(y) is the temperature in the atmosphere as a function of height, and h(t) is the height of a weather balloon as a function of time, then T(h(t)) is the temperature at the location of the weather balloon as a function of time.*

		Functions *(continued)*
High School	F-BF.2	Write arithmetic and geometric sequences both recursively and with an explicit formula, use them to model situations, and translate between the two forms.*
	F-TF.5	Choose trigonometric functions to model periodic phenomena with specified amplitude, frequency, and midline.*
	F-TF.7	(+) Use inverse functions to solve trigonometric equations that arise in modeling contexts; evaluate the solutions using technology, and interpret them in terms of the context.*
		Geometry
High School	G-SRT.8	Use trigonometric ratios and the Pythagorean Theorem to solve right triangles in applied problems.*
	G-GPE.7	Use coordinates to compute perimeters of polygons and areas of triangles and rectangles, e.g., using the distance formula.*
	G-GMD.3	Use volume formulas for cylinders, pyramids, cones, and spheres to solve problems.*
	G-MG.1	Use geometric shapes, their measures, and their properties to describe objects (e.g., modeling a tree trunk or a human torso as a cylinder).*
	G-MG.2	Apply concepts of density based on area and volume in modeling situations (e.g., persons per square mile, BTUs per cubic foot).*
	G.MG.3	Apply geometric methods to solve design problems (e.g., designing an object or structure to satisfy physical constraints or minimize cost; working with typographic grid systems based on ratios).*

High School Advanced Mathematics Standards

"The high school standards specify the mathematics that all students should study in order to be college and career ready. Additional mathematics that students should learn in order to take advanced courses such as calculus, advanced statistics, or discrete mathematics is indicated by (+), as in this example:

> *(+) Represent complex numbers on the complex plane in rectangular and polar form (including real and imaginary numbers).*

All standards without a (+) symbol should be in the common mathematics curriculum for all college and career ready students. Standards with a (+) symbol may also appear in courses intended for all students."

—CCSSI, 2010, p. 57

		Number and Quantity
High School	**N-CN.3**	**Perform arithmetic operations with complex numbers.**
		3. **(+)** Find the conjugate of a complex number; use conjugates to find moduli and quotients of complex numbers.
	N-CN.4,5,6	**Represent complex numbers and their operations on the complex plane.**
		4. **(+)** Represent complex numbers on the complex plane in rectangular and polar form (including real and imaginary numbers), and explain why the rectangular and polar forms of a given complex number represent the same number.
		5. **(+)** Represent addition, subtraction, multiplication, and conjugation of complex numbers geometrically on the complex plane; use properties of this representation for computation. *For example, $(-1 + \sqrt{3}\, i)^3 = 8$ because $(-1 + \sqrt{3}\, i)$ has modulus 2 and argument 120°.*
		6. **(+)** Calculate the distance between numbers in the complex plane as the modulus of the difference, and the midpoint of a segment as the average of the numbers at its endpoints.
	N-CN.8,9	**Use complex numbers in polynomial identities and equations.**
		8. **(+)** Extend polynomial identities to the complex numbers. *For example, rewrite $x^2 + 4$ as $(x + 2i)(x - 2i)$.*
		9. **(+)** Know the Fundamental Theorem of Algebra; show that it is true for quadratic polynomials.

		Number and Quantity *(continued)*	
High School	**N-VM.1,2,3**	**Represent and model with vector quantities.** 1. **(+)** Recognize vector quantities as having both magnitude and direction. Represent vector quantities by directed line segments, and use appropriate symbols for vectors and their magnitudes (e.g., $\mathbf{v}$, $|\mathbf{v}|$, $\|\mathbf{v}\|$, v). 2. **(+)** Find the components of a vector by subtracting the coordinates of an initial point from the coordinates of a terminal point. 3. **(+)** Solve problems involving velocity and other quantities that can be represented by vectors.

	N-VM.4,5	**Perform operations on vectors.**
		4. **(+)** Add and subtract vectors.
		   a. Add vectors end-to-end, component-wise, and by the parallelo-gram rule. Understand that the magnitude of a sum of two vectors is typically not the sum of the magnitudes.
		   b. Given two vectors in magnitude and direction form, determine the magnitude and direction of their sum.
		   c. Understand vector subtraction $\mathbf{v} - \mathbf{w}$ as $\mathbf{v} + (-\mathbf{w})$, where $-\mathbf{w}$ is the additive inverse of $\mathbf{w}$, with the same magnitude as $\mathbf{w}$ and pointing in the opposite direction. Represent vector subtraction graphically by connecting the tips in the appropriate order, and perform vector subtraction component-wise.
		5. **(+)** Multiply a vector by a scalar.
		   a. Represent scalar multiplication graphically by scaling vectors and possibly reversing their direction; perform scalar multiplication component-wise, e.g., as $c(v_x, v_y) = (cv_x, cv_y)$.
		   b. Compute the magnitude of a scalar multiple $c\mathbf{v}$ using $\|c\mathbf{v}\| = |c|\mathbf{v}$. Compute the direction of $c\mathbf{v}$ knowing that when $|c|\mathbf{v} \neq 0$, the direction of $c\mathbf{v}$ is either along $\mathbf{v}$ (for $c > 0$) or against $\mathbf{v}$ (for $c < 0$).

	N-VM.6, 7, 8, 9, 10, 11, 12	**Perform operations on matrices and use matrices in applications.** 6. **(+)** Use matrices to represent and manipulate data, e.g., to represent payoffs or incidence relationships in a network. 7. **(+)** Multiply matrices by scalars to produce new matrices, e.g., as when all of the payoffs in a game are doubled. 8. **(+)** Add, subtract, and multiply matrices of appropriate dimensions. 9. **(+)** Understand that, unlike multiplication of numbers, matrix multiplication for square matrices is not a commutative operation, but still satisfies the associative and distributive properties. 10. **(+)** Understand that the zero and identity matrices play a role in matrix addition and multiplication similar to the role of 0 and 1 in the real numbers. The determinant of a square matrix is nonzero if and only if the matrix has a multiplicative inverse. 11. **(+)** Multiply a vector (regarded as a matrix with one column) by a matrix of suitable dimensions to produce another vector. Work with matrices as transformations of vectors. 12. **(+)** Work with 2 × 2 matrices as transformations of the plane, and interpret the absolute value of the determinant in terms of area.

Algebra		
High School	**A-APR.5**	**Use polynomial identities to solve problems.** 5. (+) Know and apply the Binomial Theorem for the expansion of $(x + y)^n$ in powers of x and y for a positive integer n, where x and y are any numbers, with coefficients determined for example by Pascal's Triangle.
	A-APR.7	**Rewrite rational expressions.** 7. (+) Understand that rational expressions form a system analogous to the rational numbers, closed under addition, subtraction, multiplication, and division by a nonzero rational expression; add, subtract, multiply, and divide rational expressions.
	A-REI.8,9	**Solve systems of equations.** 8. (+) Represent a system of linear equations as a single matrix equation in a vector variable. 9. (+) Find the inverse of a matrix if it exists and use it to solve systems of linear equations (using technology for matrices of dimension 3 × 3 or greater).
Functions		
High School	**F-IF.7d**	**Analyze functions using different representations.** 7. Graph functions expressed symbolically and show key features of the graph, by hand in simple cases and using technology for more complicated cases.* d. (+) Graph rational functions, identifying zeros and asymptotes when suitable factorizations are available, and showing end behavior.
	F-BF.1c	**Build a function that models a relationship between two quantities.** 1. Write a function that describes a relationship between two quantities.* c. (+) Compose functions. *For example, if T(y) is the temperature in the atmosphere as a function of height, and h(t) is the height of a weather balloon as a function of time, then T(h(t)) is the temperature at the location of the weather balloon as a function of time.*
	F-BF.4b,c,d	**Build new functions from existing functions.** 4. Find inverse functions. b. (+) Verify by composition that one function is the inverse of another. c. (+) Read values of an inverse function from a graph or a table, given that the function has an inverse. d. (+) Produce an invertible function from a non-invertible function by restricting the domain.

		Functions *(continued)*
High School	F-BF.5	**Build new functions from existing functions.** 5. (+) Understand the inverse relationship between exponents and logarithms and use this relationship to solve problems involving logarithms and exponents.
	F-TF.3,4	**Extend the domain of trigonometric functions using the unit circle.** 3. (+) Use special triangles to determine geometrically the values of sine, cosine, tangent for $\pi/3$, $\pi/4$, and $\pi/6$, and use the unit circle to express the values of sine, cosines, and tangent for x, $\pi + x$, and $2\pi - x$ in terms of their values for x, where x is any real number. 4. (+) Use the unit circle to explain symmetry (odd and even) and periodicity of trigonometric functions.
	F-TF.6,7	**Model periodic phenomena with trigonometric functions.** 6. (+) Understand that restricting a trigonometric function to a domain on which it is always increasing or always decreasing allows its inverse to be constructed. 7. (+) Use inverse functions to solve trigonometric equations that arise in modeling contexts; evaluate the solutions using technology, and interpret them in terms of the context.*
	F-TF.9	**Prove and apply trigonometric identities.** 9. (+) Prove the addition and subtraction formulas for sine, cosine, and tangent and use them to solve problems.
		Geometry
High School	G-SRT.9,10,11	**Apply trigonometry to general triangles.** 9. (+) Derive the formula $A = 1/2\ ab \sin(C)$ for the area of a triangle by drawing an auxiliary line from a vertex perpendicular to the opposite side. 10. (+) Prove the Laws of Sines and Cosines and use them to solve problems. 11. (+) Understand and apply the Law of Sines and the Law of Cosines to find unknown measurements in right and non-right triangles (e.g., surveying problems, resultant forces).
	G-C.4	**Understand and apply theorems about circles.** 4. (+) Construct a tangent line from a point outside a given circle to the circle.
	G-GPE.3	**Translate between the geometric description and the equation for a conic section.** 3. (+) Derive the equations of ellipses and hyperbolas given the foci, using the fact that the sum or difference of distances from the foci is constant.
	G-GMD.2	**Explain volume formulas and use them to solve problems.** 2. (+) Give an informal argument using Cavalieri's principle for the formulas for the volume of a sphere and other solid figures.

Statistics and Probability		
High School	**S-CP.8,9**	**Use the rules of probability to compute probabilities of compound events in a uniform probability model.** 8. (+) Apply the general Multiplication Rule in a uniform probability model, P(A and B) = P(A)P(B|A) = P(B)P(A|B), and interpret the answer in terms of the model. 9. (+) Use permutations and combinations to compute probabilities of compound events and solve problems.
	S-MD.1,2,3,4	**Calculate expected values and use them to solve problems.** 1. (+) Define a random variable for a quantity of interest by assigning a numerical value to each event in a sample space; graph the corresponding probability distribution using the same graphical displays as for data distributions. 2. (+) Calculate the expected value of a random variable; interpret it as the mean of the probability distribution. 3. (+) Develop a probability distribution for a random variable defined for a sample space in which theoretical probabilities can be calculated; find the expected value. *For example, find the theoretical probability distribution for the number of correct answers obtained by guessing on all five questions of a multiple-choice test where each question has four choices, and find the expected grade under various grading schemes.* 4. (+) Develop a probability distribution for a random variable defined for a sample space in which probabilities are assigned empirically; find the expected value. *For example, find a current data distribution on the number of TV sets per household in the United States, and calculate the expected number of sets per household. How many TV sets would you expect to find in 100 randomly selected households?*
	S-MD.5,6,7	**Use probability to evaluate outcomes of decisions.** 5. (+) Weigh the possible outcomes of a decision by assigning probabilities to payoff values and finding expected values. a. Find the expected payoff for a game of chance. *For example, find the expected winnings from a state lottery ticket or a game at a fast-food restaurant.* b. Evaluate and compare strategies on the basis of expected values. *For example, compare a high-deductible versus a low-deductible automobile insurance policy using various, but reasonable, chances of having a minor or a major accident.* 6. (+) Use probabilities to make fair decisions (e.g., drawing by lots, using a random number generator). 7. (+) Analyze decisions and strategies using probability concepts (e.g., product testing, medical testing, pulling a hockey goalie at the end of a game).

Source: Common Core State Standards for Mathematics (CCSSI, 2010).

Index